COASTAL COOKING
with JOHN SHIELDS

Also by John Shields

The Chesapeake Bay Cookbook
Chesapeake Bay Cooking with John Shields

COASTAL COOKING

with JOHN SHIELDS

Broadway Books   New York

BROADWAY

COASTAL COOKING WITH JOHN SHIELDS. Copyright © 2004 by John Shields. All rights reserved. No part of this book may be reproduced or transmitted in any form or by any means, electronic or mechanical, including photocopying, recording, or by any information storage and retrieval system, without written permission from the publisher. For information, address Broadway Books, a division of Random House, Inc.

PRINTED IN CHINA

BROADWAY BOOKS and its logo, a letter B bisected on the diagonal, are trademarks of Random House, Inc.

Visit our website at www.broadwaybooks.com

First edition published 2004

Book design by Elizabeth Rendfleisch
Photography by David Harp/Chesapeakephotos.com

Library of Congress Cataloging-in-Publication Data
Shields, John (John Edward)
    Coastal cooking with John Shields / John Shields.— 1st ed.
        p.   cm.
    Includes index.
    1. Cookery, American. 2. Cookery (Fish) 3. Cookery (Seafood) I. Title.
TX715.S1475 2004
641.6'92—dc22

                                                                    2003063789

ISBN 0-7679-1535-6

10 9 8 7 6 5 4 3 2 1

To my dear departed culinary heroes: Frances Kitching, Alberta Reese, Mealy Sartori, Alva Crockett and, as always, Grandma Gertie—You'll always live on in the tastes, aromas, and delicious memories of your much-beloved recipes.

Contents

Acknowledgments

As with any large undertaking, there are many thanks to go around. And if you are a chef, restaurateur, and television host, that list grows exponentially. It's not easy to get away from a busy restaurant, so thanks must first go out to John Francis for keeping the home fires burning and Gertrude's up and running. My eternal gratitude to chefs Cesar Calderon and Tomislav Niksic (and kudos to Tom for fine food styling) for keeping watch in the kitchen, and to the entire staff of Gertrude's—front and back—for all the encouragement and support.

My loving and understanding family and friends gave me the time and space to collect my thoughts and recipes on these pages without too much complaining about my lack of attentiveness—my love to Mom Mom, Kathleeny, Patricia, and Lynnie.

As always my agent, Angela Miller, provided me insight and encouragement, prodding me along toward the completion of the manuscript.

My patient editor, Jennifer Josephy of Broadway Books, God love her, is a master sculptress of the written word. Allyson Giard, also of Broadway Books, kept the project on track. No matter the quality of recipes and text, all is for naught without a first-rate production team, and that we have had under the direction of production manager Kim Cacho and production editor Chris Fortunato.

My cohort and good friend in all things coastal, Karol Menzie, was the talented project manager and editorial guide for this work. Through many deadlines and malfunctioning electronic equipment, Karol not only hung in there, but helped me do the same. Karol—I love you.

I covered quite a number of miles to find all these delicious recipes, and travel-planner extraordinaire Ragan Lentz of AESU Travel in Hampden got me where I needed to go.

Many thanks to David and Barbara Harp for your outstanding images and valued friendship.

Being out on the road for many months can be lonely, but during my West Coast research trip, from San Diego to Seattle, I had with me my dear friend Mary McGowan as technical assistant, navigator, therapist, and dining partner. Mary, you are a saint!

My gratitude to those who shared their ideas and personal contacts for my research: the Florida folks, Kathy Martin and Deborah Hartz; cookbook author and all-round nice guy Steven

Raichlen; Charlyne Varkonyi-Staub; Carol Dunton of Corpus Christi and Andi Zarro of Galveston; and the West Coast contingent: Maureen Clancy, Edie Greenberg, Jon Rowley, Ron Paul, Geoff Latham, David Blandford, Heather Bryant, and Rita Kuller.

A very special thanks to Judi Strada of *San Diego* magazine, who was the best Southern California tour guide a guy could ask for.

I must also extend my gratitude to the talented group of people who work with me on my *Coastal Cooking* television series and to our production company. Abbie Kealy, producer/director, is the best; our executive producer, Mike Styer; the Kitchen Goddess and my official "keeper," Andrea Farnum; the gal with a plan, Josianne Pennington; my business partners, Pat and George Davis, and Dave and Marla Oros. Jack Gilden and the gang at Gilden Integrated gave us a great look, as did Julia Evins, our graphic designer. Also, my appreciation to Chris Funkhouser and the team at American Public Television in Boston.

Public television is a great gift to our nation, but it takes forward-thinking, responsible companies to make it possible. My heartfelt thanks to Shirley and Brice Phillips, Mark Sneed, and Honey Konicoff of Phillips Foods. Our coastal kitchen is a beautiful setting and would not be possible without the Fretz Corporation and the assistance of the lovely Jennifer Connelly Care.

And last, but really not least, Sandy Snow, for helping me distill my coastal dream.

Having grown up on the shores of the Chesapeake Bay, I have always found myself drawn to the water. Maybe it's in my blood. My great-grandfather was an Irish ship's carpenter who made his way from the Old Sod to Newfoundland, and later sailed to the Chesapeake, where he established our clan. As a little boy, I watched as my uncles handily crafted their own fishing boats. And sometimes I myself would set sail into a misty bayside morning, laying down trotlines to lure feisty blue crabs from the brackish bay waters.

While a full morning of fishing and crabbing was an adventure unto itself, the real fun would begin when we sailed back home to the waiting band of family and friends at the dock. Our triumphant catch was merely an

1 INTRODUCTION

addition to a summertime Chesapeake Bay feast already under way. Slightly sunburned cousins and aunts sat at picnic tables, husking bushels of freshly picked sweet Silver Queen corn. My grandmother Gertie would be hovering over a giant pot of country-style crab soup, chock-full of the local farms' produce: onions, vine-ripened tomatoes, carrots, lima beans, and tender sweet peas. Our overflowing baskets of newly fished blue crabs were somehow all layered into the family's one enormous black enamel crab pot, and soon the aroma of steaming crabs and the Chesapeake's ubiquitous seafood seasoning wafted through the humid summer breeze. I still remember lying in the old canvas army hammock that was securely fastened between two tall oaks, the feast and revelry continuing around me, being thankful for what an amazing life I had. These childhood experiences on the Bay became the foundation for my lifelong love of food, nature, and community.

After my college years, the wanderlust of youth inspired me to set out for New England, and there I settled with friends in an old, gray-shingled, waterside bungalow on Cape Cod, Massachusetts. I began my culinary career as a restaurant chef and soon encountered all manner of "foreign" seafood and crustaceans. Each day at the kitchen's delivery door, local fishermen offered crates brimming with glistening cod, meticulously filleted scrod, succulent bay scallops, baskets of shiny black mussels with beards still intact, and, to my horror, containers of still-quivering squid. This definitely was not the Chesapeake.

While living on the Cape, I continued to learn, wrestling down more than my share of giant lobsters and shucking countless gallons of clams for fabled New England clam chowder. And I found the people of New England to be just as interesting as the food. Many of the folks who worked the water were of Portuguese descent, such as Ursula Silva and her husband, Big Clem (men are very important in Portuguese kitchens), Cape Cod versions of my grandmother Gertie. In their kitchen I witnessed the same love of cooking I had experienced as a child. Clem and Ursie's Portuguese Squid Stew, a re-creation of Big Clem's garlicky and rich tomato-based stew, thick with chunks of white potatoes and a flotilla of simmering squid fresh from the bay, is served in gigantic ceramic bowls along with freshly baked, crusty Portuguese bread. The aroma of the stew, images of moonlit Cape Cod dunes, and the sound of crashing waves will be with me forever.

Wanderlust took hold of me again (it must be my great-grandfather's fault), and off I ventured to the Promised Land of northern California and the San Francisco Bay. Utter amazement is all I can recall on my arrival where the choppy waters of the San Francisco Bay collide with the Pacific Ocean at the Golden Gate Bridge, surrounded by lush mountains and foothills bejeweled with towns. I lived in a castle (a faux one, but a castle nevertheless!) situated high up in the hills, where every day I woke to a view of the entire Bay Area. After nearly twenty years there, I never once tired of the breathtaking vistas, truly awed by the splendor of nature.

Now, that was just the landscape—then there was the food! This East Coast kid had never seen anything like it. I could step out into my California yard and pick fresh lemons, figs, and avocados. In town were huge markets dedicated entirely to the largest assortment of fruits, vegetables, lettuces, nuts, and legumes that I had ever seen in my life.

I worked as the chef of a small French restaurant with a daily-changing menu, dependent on the seasonal market. As the chef, I felt like a kid in a candy store with this array of tantalizing choices. Local fishmongers introduced me to a whole new world of seafood: Dungeness crab (they're furry!) lumbering around in tanks of salt water; Delta (California, that is) crayfish; innumerable varieties of farm-raised oysters from the cold waters of Bodega Bay and the Northern California coast; hand-harvested abalone that we would pound thin, gently sauté, and bathe with a delicate lemon butter; and quail, squab, and guinea hen, all raised and processed by a former opera singer. It was a world of culinary magic and abundance. It was also the dawn of the New American Food renaissance, led by the high priestess Alice Waters at her North Berkeley restaurant, Chez Panisse. Local San Francisco Bay area farmers grew delicate baby lettuces, while regional artisanal cheese makers began making cheeses to rival Europe's finest. It was a time of excitement, creativity, and passion, the likes of which may never again be matched.

In the San Francisco Bay area, the availability of ethnic cuisines from which to draw inspiration for a chef or a serious home cook is unparalleled. The region's Asian markets and shopping districts, serving the largest Asian population out- side mainland China and Hong Kong, almost enable one to take a trip to the Orient for the price of a city bus ticket. Mahogany-colored Peking ducks adorn poultry market windows, and stalls of Asian vegetables of every conceivable shape and variety are in abundance. The international spice route makes a stop in the Bay Area, offering fragrant herbs and spices specially blended for Cambodian, Thai, Cantonese, Mandarin, Laotian, and Vietnamese dishes. The area's thriving Latino communities fashion California's myriad of food products into tradi- tional Hispanic fare. I had always heard that America is the world's melting pot, but it never became so vibrant for me until I lived and cooked in the Bay Area.

Somehow, through some sort of marvelous culinary osmosis, I absorbed the flavors, tastes, techniques, and cultural heritages of all the wondrous cuisines that thrive in the Bay Area. I often refer to my time in San Francisco as complet- ing my "Tri-Bay" cooking experience. And that is when I returned to the food of my childhood.

Seeing the love and care with which other regional chefs were rediscovering their cuisines, I immersed myself in my Chesapeake culinary heritage. I opened a restaurant in Berkeley that specialized in the cooking of my youth. Gertie's Chesapeake Bay Café allowed me to share the food and culinary heritage on which I was weaned with the folks on the West Coast.

Later on, I took my passion a step further, going home for a year to research and write my first book, *The Chesapeake Bay Cookbook*. I traversed the expanse of the Chesapeake and its tributaries, visiting small towns, villages, waterside com- munities, and historic cities. It is true what they say about often not realizing what we have right in our own backyard, and that sabbatical year was one of the great experiences of my life. The release of that cookbook led to numerous media appearances, which in turn led me to the next juncture in my life path: another cookbook, *Chesapeake Bay Cooking with John Shields*, and a cooking series on public television.

I have journeyed full circle, having come home (in many ways) to the Chesapeake, where I now live and operate my restaurant, Gertrude's, at the Baltimore Museum of Art, a tribute to the Chesapeake and, once again, to my grandmother.

During these past years I have had the opportunity to travel, visit a bit, and cook with many communities around this vast country. And while each place has its own special qualities, it is no surprise that I am particularly drawn to the spots that are situated in coastal areas. Whether it is because of my upbringing, or simply the fact that most of civilization's great cultural, spiritual, economic, and gastronomic centers have been on the water, I just cannot get enough of the coastal life. I find myself fascinated by waterside communities and the folks who are connected to the water. After exploring and chronicling the tidewater reaches of the Chesapeake Bay in *Chesapeake Bay Cooking with John Shields*, along with the companion public television series, I decided to set sail once again and take a culinary odyssey along the magnificent coastlines of the United States.

Coastal Cooking with John Shields is a cookbook, of course, but also a series of culinary snapshots of my travels, explorations, discoveries, interactions, and impressions of the people and communities who comprise the fabric of U.S. coastal regions. As I began to plan my research and travel for this book and a companion television series, I had the romantic notion of hauling the old Airstream out of storage and traveling the highways and back roads that traverse the coastline of the United States. However, after some deliberation, I decided to fly into specific regions, rent myself a car, and from there set out to get the feel of my host town. I made numerous phone calls to long-lost family and friends all around the coasts to get contacts and recommendations on the town's best cooks—and often for a place to hang my hat for several days.

Over the past year, I wandered my way through the Carolinas to Key West and over to the Gulf through Alabama, Mississippi, Louisiana, and Texas. It was then off to the West Coast, landing in San Diego, California, and driving all the way up the incredible Pacific coast. I stopped to visit cities, towns, resorts, and parks along the way to Seattle. I hopped a plane to the Hawaiian Islands, where I sunned myself and ate way too much. Back on the mainland, I finished the whirlwind tour with a drive from Maine home to Baltimore.

As I made my rounds along the coasts, I stopped to meet each town's extraordinary cooks and storytellers. Our featured personalities are chefs, fishermen, farmers, and, most important, home cooks. These are the folks who know and live their cuisine. I have tried to balance the book with both food professionals—luminaries in their fields, whether cooks or food producers—and just plain folk. If we want to understand and truly appreciate a coastal region, these are the people to whom we need to listen.

It was a coastal culinary whirlwind, and now it seems barely a dream. Fortunately, as a reminder, I have a treasure trove of unbelievable recipes, an address book full of new friends—and a few extra pounds. With more than 125 scrumptious recipes, great stories, and fantastic new cooking friends—what's next? It's time for a new public television series, where I and friends I met along the way can reunite to share coastal recipes, techniques, tall tales . . . and some great food. So get out your pots and pans and come along with us for a guided tour of Coastal Cooking in America.

Soups and one-pot recipes are the staple of all regional cuisines. (And it just so happens they are my personal favorite dishes to prepare.) Not only is a hearty pot of soup or stew heart- and tummy-warming, but it is fairly simple to prepare. There are just a few basic variations in the preparations. There are clear and cream soups, potato-laced chowders, and seafood- or meat-and-vegetable-laden stews and gumbos, with many based on those wonderful culinary standbys, the stocks. But there's an eye-popping amount of diversity in the actual dishes, because anything and everything can and does go into a soup pot—everything from seafood and shellfish to

2 SOUPS AND ONE-POTS

fruits and vegetables, steak and lobster, cheese and nuts. Some soups and one-pots are forever wed to their regions because of particular ingredients—clam chowder in New England, she-crabs in Savannah, shellfish and okra in

Southern gumbos, fish and seafood in San Francisco's fresh-catch-in-a-bowl cioppino. Some are the result of innovative cooks and chefs using what's on hand, be it elegant or earthy—squid on Cape Cod, tiny ridgeback shrimp in Santa Barbara, saffron-infused leeks and potatoes in Portland, cantaloupes on Maryland's Eastern Shore.

The idea of making stock gives some people anxiety attacks, but homemade stocks are culinary gold in the refrigerator or freezer—they're basic to soups and stews, and they are the flavor and structural base for a stunning array of other dishes, from sauces to sautés to grains and stuffings. It's well worth the small trouble of making stock for the burst of flavor it imparts to every dish it's used in. There's a wide range of traditional and not-so-usual dishes in this chapter as you wander your culinary way up and down the coasts of this great soup-loving country.

This soup was originally made from female blue crabs and their delectable orange roe. Many states now have restrictions on catching female crabs, but this soup holds its own as a first-class cream of crab if you substitute a pound of crabmeat for the she-crabs.

Savannah She-Crab Soup

Even the locals now take short-cuts. Helen Jackson, a dear family friend from Savannah, Georgia, says: "I stopped picking the crab years ago when my fingers got too stiff, but now I cheat a bit and use a pound of jumbo crabmeat. If there's not any orangey roe in the meat, I use a few hard-boiled egg yolks and chop 'em up and then add it to the soup when it's finished cooking. My friends always say it's their favorite crab soup—and they don't even know there's egg in there."

A number of Southern cooks I have spoken with prepare their she-crab soup in a double boiler because it is important not to bring the soup to a boil. I find that as long as one is careful, and tends the pot, the direct method works well.

Serves 6 to 8

12 live female blue crabs, or
   1 pound crabmeat, picked
   over
8 tablespoons (1 stick) butter
1 small onion, finely diced
4 tablespoons all-purpose
   flour
2 cups Fish Stock (recipe
   follows)
2 cups heavy whipping cream
1 tablespoon Worcestershire
   sauce
1/8 teaspoon Tabasco
Pinch of ground mace
   (optional)
1 teaspoon salt
Pinch of ground white
   pepper
1/4 cup dry sherry
Juice of 1/2 lemon
2 teaspoons finely minced
   shallot
1/2 cup heavy whipping cream
   with 1 tablespoon dry
   sherry, lightly whipped, for
   garnish
Cayenne pepper, for garnish

If you are using live crabs, fill a stock pot large enough to easily accommodate the crabs halfway with lightly salted water and bring to a boil. Add the crabs, cover, and allow to cook for 15 minutes. Remove the crabs from the pot and rinse with cool water to bring down the temperature. When the crabs are cool enough to handle, pick out the meat and orange roe and set aside.

Melt 4 tablespoons of the butter in a large, heavy-bottomed saucepan over medium heat, add the onion, and sauté until tender, about 5 minutes. Whisk in the flour and cook over medium heat, stirring constantly, for 2 to 3 minutes. It is important to remain with the soup at this point, taking care not to brown the mixture. Remove from the heat and slowly whisk in the stock and the cream. Add the Worcestershire and Tabasco and return the saucepan to medium heat, stirring frequently until the mixture thickens, about 20 minutes. Add the mace (if

using), salt, pepper, sherry, and lemon juice. Simmer for 20 minutes longer and remove from the heat.

Heat the remaining 4 tablespoons of butter in a sauté pan over medium-high heat. Add the shallot and sauté for about 1 minute. Add the reserved crabmeat and roe, or the pound of crabmeat. Heat for 1 to 2 minutes, tossing the crabmeat in the butter to coat evenly. Add the crabmeat mixture to the soup and reheat until hot.

Ladle into soup bowls and top with the sherried whipped cream and a very light sprinkling of cayenne.

Fish Stock

Makes about 2 quarts

3 1/2 to 4 pounds fish heads, bones, and trimmings (see note)
2 onions, peeled and sliced
4 celery stalks, chopped
2 carrots, chopped
4 garlic cloves, unpeeled and crushed
2 teaspoons whole black peppercorns
2 bay leaves
2 teaspoons dried thyme
4 sprigs parsley
1 cup dry white wine

Rinse the fish well in cold water. Place all ingredients in a large stock pot. Add 10 cups cold water, or more as needed, making sure the liquid rises about one inch over the top of the bones, and bring to a boil. Reduce heat and simmer, uncovered, for 30 minutes. Remove from heat and let stand for 15 to 20 minutes, skimming off the surface foam frequently. Strain through a fine sieve or cheesecloth. Cool completely and refrigerate if not using immediately.

NOTES ON FISH STOCK: White-fleshed fish such as members of the flatfish family—sole, flounder, halibut, as well as snapper and rockfish—make an excellent fish stock. It is always a good idea to make a large batch of fish stock at a time as it freezes nicely. A friend of mine takes part of her stock, reduces it by half the volume, freezes it in ice cube trays, and stores the cubes in zippered plastic freezer bags. By thinking ahead, she always has a concentrated fish stock ready to go, and it does not take up too much of her freezer space.

SAVANNAH, GEORGIA

Savannah, Georgia, founded in 1733 by British General James Oglethorpe, has been famous for a long time, first for its deep-water port, second for being a "Christmas present" to Abe Lincoln from General William Tecumseh Sherman in 1864, and third for its 1950s-urban-stagnation-turned-1970s-historic-renovation triumph. All that was long before John Berendt celebrated the city's essential quirkiness in *Midnight in the Garden of Good and Evil* in 1994. His tale of murder, mayhem, larceny, voodoo, and general weirdness put Savannah resolutely on the map for most Americans. The truth is, Savannah has long been hospitable to artists, sailors, tourists, eccentrics, entrepreneurs, and grande dames. The trees dripping with Spanish moss, the gorgeous historic houses on their neat squares, all bathed in a sultry humidity, are a backdrop for a place where anything can happen, and often does.

On a chilly day with the winds blowing in the fall or winter, this is the best stew on earth. There are all sorts of recipes for oyster stews, but the people who live and work the water know that simple is the way to go. The oysters need to be allowed to shine through. This recipe from Williamsburg, Virginia, where King George III perpetually reigns, combines the briny oysters of Tidewater Virginia, with the salty, smoky flavor of Virginia's world-famous Smithfield ham.

Colonial Williamsburg Oyster Stew

Serves 2

4 tablespoons (1/2 stick) butter
1 tablespoon minced Smithfield ham, or other dried salty ham
1/2 pint oysters, with their liquor
2 cups half-and-half, heated (see note)
1 teaspoon Worcestershire sauce
Pinch of salt
Paprika, for garnish

In a large saucepan, melt 2 tablespoons of the butter and sauté the ham for 1 minute. Add the oysters and reserved liquor, and cook on medium heat for 3 minutes, or until edges of oysters just begin to curl. Do not allow to boil! Add the hot half-and-half, Worcestershire, and salt, and bring almost to the boil. Serve hot, garnished with pats of the remaining butter and a little paprika.

NOTE: Using heated half-and-half reduces the cooking time, and thus reduces the risk of overcooking the oysters.

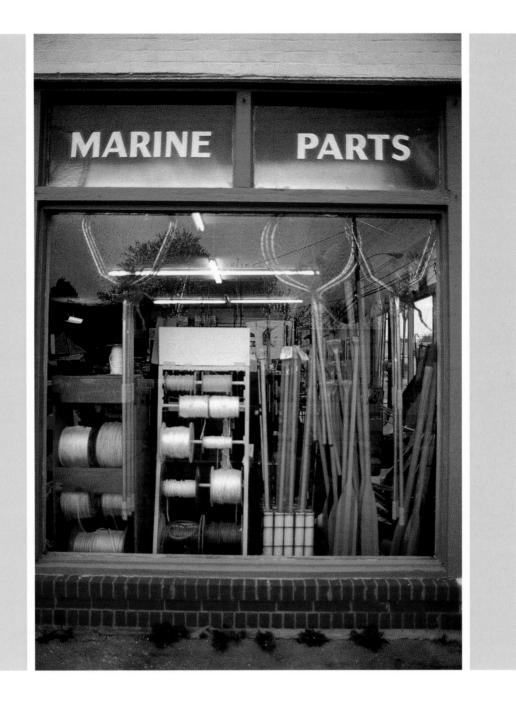

COLONIAL WILLIAMSBURG, VIRGINIA

From 1699 to 1780, Williamsburg on the James River in Tidewater Virginia was the state capital, a thriving metropolis of shops, churches, and homes elegant and humble. It was a hotbed of fashion and politics, commerce and society. When the capital was moved to Richmond, Williamsburg for the next 150 years was just a sleepy college town. Then, in 1926, a local resident, Rev. Dr. D.A.R. Goodwin, anxious to preserve the area's history, interested philanthropist John D. Rockefeller Jr. in the idea of saving as much of the town's Colonial fabric as possible. Dr. Goodwin's ideas were modest, but the project bloomed, and eventually about 85 percent of the original area of the capital was drawn under the preservation-restoration umbrella. More than eighty buildings have been restored, along with their gardens, outbuildings, roads, and other accoutrements.

Walking around Colonial Williamsburg today is like stepping into a time machine and being transported back to Colonial times. The restoration has been meticulous and includes everything from furniture and clothing to shop signage, paint colors, and plants and animals. The town is "inhabited" by shopkeepers, soldiers, housewives, farmers, and others who go about their daily lives as if it were the early 1700s. They're all actors, but the illusion is perfect. The private, not-for-profit Colonial Williamsburg Foundation runs the historic area and sponsors all kinds of educational, historical, and archaeological programs, as well as operating for-profit hotels and other facilities. Recent programs have focused on the roles of Native Americans and Afro-Americans in the Williamsburg story. And what about those nice-looking "Colonial" homes that aren't open to the public, yet complement the streetscape in every way? They're lived in by real twenty-first-century people who give up cars, clotheslines, satellite dishes, swing sets, aluminum siding, and every other modern convenience that would destroy the authentic look, for the sake of preserving the image. As a result, they live, before and after hours, in one of the loveliest and most serene spots in the coastal community.

These small (less than two inches long) shrimp are native to the California coastal waters between Monterey Bay and Cedros Island in Baja, and are a popular menu item in Southern California. Even though petite, they have a delightfully sweet flavor. At Santa Barbara's popular eatery, Bouchon, the chefs have a grand time preparing the delicacy in several ways, including this hearty chowder and delightful pot stickers. Ridgeback shrimp are primarily sold fresh, head on. If you can't make it over to Santa Barbara, Bouchon owner Mitchell Sjerven says that just about any shrimp will work beautifully in the recipe. However, if you consider yourself a shrimp purist, it's not a bad reason to take a trip to Santa Barbara.

Ridgeback Shrimp and Sweet Corn Chowder

Serves 4 to 6

1^1/4 pounds Santa Barbara ridgeback or other shrimp, peeled and deveined
4 tablespoons vegetable oil or olive oil
^{1}/2 cup white wine
3 ounces pancetta, diced (see note)
1 large white onion, diced
1 celery stalk, diced
^{1}/2 cup diced red pepper
6 garlic cloves, minced
^{1}/2 cup all-purpose flour
4 cups Fish Stock (page 10) or Chicken Stock (page 35)
2 large waxy yellow potatoes, such as Yukon Gold, peeled and diced
4 ears of corn, kernels cut from cob
1 bay leaf
1 teaspoon chopped fresh thyme
1^1/2 cups milk
^{1}/2 cup heavy cream
Salt and freshly ground black pepper
^{1}/4 to ^{1}/2 teaspoon Worcestershire sauce, or to taste

In a large skillet, sauté all the shrimp in 2 tablespoons of the oil for 3 to 4 minutes or until cooked through. Remove the shrimp from the skillet. Reserve 4 to 6 whole shrimp and cut the rest into pieces. Add the white wine to the pan and scrape up the browned bits of shrimp. Reserve liquid for soup.

Put the remaining 2 tablespoons of oil in a soup pot and cook the pancetta until crisp. Remove the pancetta, then add the onion, celery, red pepper, and garlic. Cook the vegetables until the onion is translucent. Whisk in the flour, a little at a time, to make a roux. Cook for about 3 minutes, whisking constantly; do not let the mixture brown. Add the stock and reserved shrimp-wine liquid. Add the potatoes, corn, bay leaf, and thyme and simmer until potatoes are soft.

In a separate pan, heat the milk and cream until hot but not boiling; pour into the soup, stirring constantly. Add the chopped shrimp. Season to taste with salt, pepper, and Worcestershire sauce, and continue to cook until mixture is hot. Ladle into individual bowls and garnish with the reserved whole shrimp.

NOTE: Pancetta is unsmoked Italian bacon. If you can't find it, substitute unsmoked bacon.

This is it—the real thing—pure, unadulterated, classic New England chowder, rich with clams, lightly enhanced with cream, and fragrant with briny broth. I have simplified the recipe a bit—no shucking your own basket of clams and reserving the wonderful juices by straining them through layers of cheesecloth. You can have your fishmonger do this. The recipe will make an outstanding chowder for family and friends. The original versions do not use flour but made a paste of crushed oyster crackers and water to bind the juices a bit. This modern version is much easier.

Back Bay Clam Chowder

Serves 6 to 8

One 3-inch cube salt pork, diced

1 large onion, finely diced

5 tablespoons all-purpose flour

4 cups potatoes (3 to 4 potatoes), peeled and cut into $3/4$-inch cubes

1 quart chopped clams, juice reserved

4 cups milk

Salt and freshly ground black pepper

Freshly chopped parsley, for garnish (optional)

Put the salt pork in a large, heavy-bottomed saucepan and cook over medium heat until the fat is rendered. Discard the rind. Add the onion to the fat in the pot and sauté for 5 minutes or until soft. Add the flour and cook over medium heat for 3 minutes, stirring constantly, taking care not to brown the flour. Stir in the potatoes and add clam juice mixed with enough water to just barely cover the potatoes. Simmer for 20 minutes, or until potatoes are cooked through. In a saucepan, heat the milk until tiny bubbles appear around the sides of the pan. Add the hot milk and the chopped clams to the pot and continue to simmer gently for 10 minutes more. Season to taste with salt and pepper. Garnish with freshly chopped parsley and serve with oyster crackers.

NOTES ON PREPARATION: Take care when adding salt as the clams themselves, as well as their juices, can be quite salty depending upon where they were harvested. I generally prefer to add $1/2$ teaspoon of fresh whole thyme to my chowder, but it is not part of the traditional recipe.

It seems Long Island, New York, and Manhattan have argued for some time over just who gets credit for developing this recipe. Although some Long Islanders—who just can't let go—still refer to the chowder as Long Island Clam Chowder, the rest of the culinary world is in agreement that it is a Big Apple version. The chowder reminds me stylistically of a Maryland vegetable crab soup, with a vegetable soup base flavored with shellfish, and is totally satisfying. I realize that most people prefer a cream-based clam chowder, but I'll wholeheartedly cast my ballot for the vegetable rendition.

Big Apple Clam Chowder

Serves 6 to 8

One 2-inch piece salt pork or
 $^1/_4$ cup bacon drippings
1 small onion, diced
1 celery stalk, diced
1 small green bell pepper,
 seeded and diced
1 medium carrot, diced
2 teaspoons minced garlic
2 cups stewed tomatoes, or
 canned diced tomatoes
$^1/_2$ teaspoon oregano
$^1/_2$ teaspoon dried thyme
2 medium potatoes, peeled
 and diced
4 cups chopped clams, juice
 reserved
Tabasco Sauce
Salt and freshly ground black
 pepper

Render the salt pork or heat the bacon drippings in a large, heavy-bottomed saucepan. (If using salt pork, remove the rind.) Add the onion and sauté for 5 minutes. Add the celery, bell pepper, carrot, and garlic, and sauté until slightly softened, 8 to 10 minutes. Add the stewed tomatoes, reserved clam juice (you need about 6 cups of clam juice—if there is not sufficient juice from the clams, add water to the reserved juice), oregano, and thyme. Cook over medium heat for about 15 minutes. Add the potatoes and continue cooking, stirring occasionally, for about 30 minutes or until potatoes are just tender. Add the clams and gently simmer for 10 minutes longer. Do not overcook the clams or they will toughen. Season with Tabasco and salt and pepper to taste. Serve with soda or oyster crackers.

TABASCO SAUCE   This condiment carries such cachet among devotees that they are known for carrying tiny vials of it with them at all times. First developed in the 1860s by Edmund McIlhenny on Louisiana's Avery Island, Tabasco Sauce is made today as it was then, of red pepper, vinegar, and salt indigenous to the "salt-dome" island that is Avery Island. It's aged for up to three years in white-oak barrels—rather like fine wine, or even single-malt Scotch. And the name? Tabasco is said to be a Native American word meaning—what else for a sauce that sets your taste buds aflame?—"land where the soil is hot and humid."

Tangier Island, Virginia, is a remote outpost in the middle of the Chesapeake Bay, not far from where the Bay merges with the Atlantic Ocean. It's not a place for the faint of heart, for the elements can at times be quite unforgiving. When the cold winds of winter blow,

Tangier Island Sea Clam Chowder with Dough Boys

one understands why chowders were originally created—they warm you through and through. This chowder is a version of one I learned from Alva Crockett, the five-time mayor of Tangier, and the great-great-grandson of Davy Crockett. Alva always used the large sea clams, shucking them himself and reserving their briny liquor. There is no flour used to thicken the soup—only potatoes and Alva's "dough boys." Another ingredient that may appear to be missing is the milk. Alva scolds, "Milk is for babies and cereal, not for chowders." In this case, the man's right.

Serves 8 to 10

4 tablespoons bacon fat
2 onions, finely diced
4 large potatoes, peeled and cubed
4 cups chopped clams, fresh, frozen, or canned, with juice reserved
Salt and freshly ground black pepper
Dough Boys (recipe follows)

Heat the bacon fat in a stock pot over medium heat and sauté the onions until tender. Add the potatoes and the reserved clam juice. Add enough water to just barely cover the potatoes. Cook uncovered for about 30 minutes or until potatoes can be pierced with a knife. Add the chopped clams and, if necessary, a bit more clam juice or water to just cover the potato-clam mixture. Reduce heat and simmer for 20 minutes more, or until clams are tender. Season to taste with salt and pepper. Let the chowder rest for at least 30 minutes before serving.

When ready to serve, place the chowder back on the stove and return to medium heat. When mixture is quite hot, place the Dough Boys on top of the bubbling chowder. Place a lid on the pot and continue to simmer for 15 minutes, or until Dough Boys have puffed up. Serve in bowls with plenty of bread.

Alva's Dough Boys

2 cups all-purpose flour
4 teaspoons baking powder
1 teaspoon salt
4 tablespoons solid
  shortening (or lard)
$1/2$ cup milk

Sift together the flour, baking powder, and salt into a large bowl. Work in the shortening with your fingertips or a pastry blender until the mixture is the consistency of coarse meal. Combine the milk with $1/2$ cup water and beat into the flour with a spoon until a stiff (not wet) dough is formed. Turn out the dough onto a lightly floured surface and knead gently for 1 minute. Return to bowl and cover with a towel until ready to use.

To form the Dough Boys, pull silver-dollar-size pieces of dough off the ball and roll in the palms of your hands to form rounded balls. Place the pieces on a lightly floured platter and cover with a towel until ready to use. This recipe also makes a quite respectable biscuit and will yield about one dozen.

TANGIER ISLAND, VIRGINIA

Three miles long and one mile wide, Tangier Island, Virginia, sits in the middle of Chesapeake Bay about six miles south of the Maryland-Virginia line. It was visited by Captain John Smith in 1608, but was not settled until sometime afterward. Early settlers may have been farmers; it wasn't until the mid-nineteenth century that the seafood industry really took off.

Because the population has always been small and close-knit, many of the residents are related in some way, and a few family names predominate. The island isn't completely isolated—there are several ferries that bring around 500 visitors a day in summer. But islands do have language signatures—think of Australia and New Zealand, or Sicily—and that's why, tiny as it is, Tangier Island has a fascination in some rarefied academic circles because of the way the people speak. Their ancestors were from the west of England, where accents tend to be burred, and this speech has been preserved among island natives. It's said that this so-called "Tidewater" accent is the closest we can get to hearing the English of Shakespearean times.

Here we have a great party soup. It takes a bit of time to steam and remove the mussels from their shells and then to prepare the chowder, but it can, and should be, made a day ahead for maximum flavor. Rawle Jeffards and his brother Ian of Penn Cove Shellfish, on Whidbey Island, Washington, maintain that this chowder—chock-full of meaty mussels—"definitely tastes better the second day."

Whidbey Island Mussel Chowder

On the day of the party, simply reheat—cooking slowly, not allowing the soup to boil, and stirring often. A good idea for serving is to keep the chowder on the stove at a very low setting (or use diffused heat), put out a stack of bowls or oversized mugs, some serving utensils—don't forget a ladle in the pot—and let everyone serve themselves. I find guests always gravitate to the kitchen no matter where you plan to serve the meal.

Serves 12 to 14

5 pounds mussels, cleaned and debearded
1 cup white wine
1 tablespoon minced garlic
$^1/_2$ pound salt pork, finely diced
$1^1/_2$ sticks butter
3 large onions, cut in $^1/_2$-inch dice
2 cups all-purpose flour
$1^1/_2$ gallons liquid, which includes the mussel steaming liquid and water; you may also add some clam broth, if desired
1 cup celery, cut into small dice
2 pounds white potatoes (about 6 russet potatoes), diced
1 tablespoon chopped fresh thyme
Salt and freshly ground black pepper
2 cups cream

Working in batches, steam the mussels in the white wine, 1 cup water, and garlic, dividing the liquids equally among the batches. Steam until the mussels open. (Discard any that don't open.) Remove the mussels from the pot, reserving the liquid. Remove the mussel meat from the shells and place in the refrigerator until ready to use.

Strain the steaming liquid through a fine sieve or a sieve lined with cheesecloth and set aside.

Cook the salt pork in a skillet over medium heat until crisp. Set aside.

Melt the butter in a large saucepan. Add the rendered pork fat. Sauté the onions for a couple of minutes in the butter. Off the heat, add the flour, stirring well. It will make a stiff mixture. Add a third of the liquid (2 quarts), and stir to remove any lumps of flour. Return to medium heat and add the remaining liquid. Continue to stir as the soup cooks. It will thicken at this time, and it is important to stir so lumps do not appear. Bring soup just to the boil, reduce heat, and simmer for 20 minutes.

Add the salt pork, celery, potatoes, and thyme and continue cooking for 40 minutes or until potatoes are tender. While the soup is cooking, coarsely chop the mussels. Add the mussels, salt and pepper to taste, and the cream and simmer for 10 minutes.

There are few soups more elegant than lobster bisque. These days most bisques are prepared just like any other cream soup, but actually traditional bisques are thickened with rice, which gives a distinctly different texture than the flour-thickened versions. I've had wonderful lobster bisques around the country, but my favorite has always been from Maine. Perhaps there is just something about the partaking of the fragrant bisque in the gorgeous Maine countryside.

Bar Harbor Lobster Bisque

Serves 6 to 8

FOR THE LOBSTER:

1 onion, sliced
1 medium carrot, chopped
2 celery stalks, chopped
1/2 bunch parsley
2 teaspoons salt
1 teaspoon whole black
  peppercorns
1 teaspoon dried thyme
One 2-pound lobster

FOR THE BISQUE:

4 tablespoons (1/2 stick)
  butter
1 small onion, finely diced
1 leek, quartered, rinsed, and
  diced
1 carrot, peeled and diced
1 celery stalk, diced
3 tablespoons brandy
1/2 cup white rice, uncooked
1 teaspoon salt
1 1/2 cups heavy whipping
  cream
Pinch of freshly grated
  nutmeg
Cayenne pepper, for garnish
4 tablespoons minced chives,
  for garnish

COOK THE LOBSTER: Place 8 cups cold water in a stock pot with the sliced onion, carrot, celery, parsley, salt, black peppercorns, and thyme. Bring to a boil and place the lobster in the pot. Cover and boil for 20 minutes. Remove the lobster from the pot and set aside to cool. Strain the cooking liquid and set aside. When the lobster is cool, remove the meat from the shell and claws, chop the meat into bite-size pieces, and set aside. Break up the shells and claws into small pieces. Place in a food processor fitted with the steel chopping blade. Chop the shell and reserve.

PREPARE THE BISQUE: Heat the butter in a large, heavy-bottomed saucepan and sauté the onion for several minutes. Add the leek, carrot, and celery and continue to sauté for 6 minutes. Add the lobster shells and brandy, and cook for 5 minutes longer. Pour in 5 cups of the reserved lobster broth and bring to a boil. Reduce heat and cook for 20 minutes. Add the rice and salt and cook for 30 to 35 minutes, or until rice is thoroughly cooked. Remove pot from the heat and blend batches of the bisque in a blender or food processor and pass through a fine strainer. Return strained bisque to the cleaned pot and add the cream. Heat until very hot, but not boiling. Add the chopped lobster meat and a pinch of nutmeg. Gently simmer for 10 minutes longer. Adjust seasonings. Bisque may be served right away or reheated later. Garnish the bisque with a very light dusting of cayenne and sprinkle on the chives.

BAR HARBOR, MAINE

Bar Harbor, Maine, sits on the east coast of Mt. Desert Island, surrounded on three sides by the 47,633-acre Acadia National Park and on the other side by the ocean. There's evidence the island was lived on 5,000 years ago, but despite the beauty of the hilly "rock-bound" setting, the soil is too thin and poor for farming. Instead, early and late settlers came for the bounty of the sea. Bar Harbor was "discovered" in the mid-1850s by a pair of celebrity painters of the Hudson River School, Thomas Cole and Frederic Church, who came for the clear light and lush landscapes and seascapes. Their paintings drew other visitors, and for a time into the twentieth century, the town was known as a playground of the rich and famous. Today it's a study in contrasts, home to lobstermen and jet-setters, a destination for sailors and cross-country skiers, friendly to yachts and bicycles, offering knotty-pine family diners and fine antique-laden inns—there's something for everyone. There's also lobster for everyone—roasted, baked, boiled, stir-fried, served in soups, chowders, and sandwiches— heaven for fans of these particular crustaceans. And oh, yes, don't forget the blueberry pie.

My friend Clem Silva and his sister Deb have now taken the wonderful home cooking of their mom and dad (Big Clem and Ursie) and showcased it in their very own, wildly successful Provincetown, Massachusetts, eatery, called Clem & Ursie's. As far as squid stews go, the best-of-the-best are found on Cape Cod, where for hundreds of years Portuguese settlers' descendants have lived and worked the waters of the North Atlantic and prolific Cape Cod Bay.

Clem and Ursie's Squid Stew

This recipe is amazingly simple (once you've cleaned the squid) and totally satisfying. It's a great one-pot meal on a cool evening, with a bottle of full-bodied red wine, a rustic loaf of bread, and Patti Page softly singing "Old Cape Cod" in the background. It is a good idea to make this stew at least several hours before serving so that the flavors meld.

Serves 6 to 8

3 pounds prepared squid
3 tablespoons olive oil
3 onions, finely diced
2 tablespoons finely chopped garlic
1 tablespoon crushed red pepper
4 ripe tomatoes, cored and chopped
2 tablespoons tomato paste
6 medium potatoes, peeled and diced
1 tablespoon salt
2 tablespoons red wine vinegar

Clean and wash the squid thoroughly and cut into two-inch pieces.

Heat the olive oil in a large saucepan. Add the onions, garlic, and red pepper and sauté over medium heat for about 5 minutes. Add the squid, tomatoes, tomato paste, and 2 cups water. Bring to a boil, reduce the heat, and simmer for about 2 hours, or until the squid is somewhat tender. Add the potatoes and salt and continue cooking until the potatoes are tender, about 30 to 40 minutes. Add the vinegar and cook 2 minutes longer.

Okra is not found in every gumbo, although technically it should be since gumbo is an African name for okra. Gumbos come in all shapes and sizes, varying degrees of spiciness, and multiple combinations of main ingredients—seafood, poultry, and meat. A good gumbo begins with a dark, nutty-flavored roux. Cooks in the back reaches of Louisiana are known for their signature roux. I like my roux to be a reddish dark-brown, like the color of a rusty nail. However, some folks I know cook their molten roux until it is almost black—yet without a trace of a burnt flavor. Experiment until you find the roux that is right for you. This recipe feeds a crowd, which is a good idea, because it takes almost as much effort to make gumbo to feed two as to feed twenty.

Bayou Seafood Gumbo

Serves 12 to 15

1 pound live crayfish (see note)
1 cup vegetable oil
1 cup all-purpose flour
1 large onion, chopped
1 cup chopped celery
1 green bell pepper, seeded, diced
1 cup finely chopped green onions
3 tablespoons minced garlic
3 cups peeled and chopped ripe fresh tomatoes, or 3 cans (16-ounce each) diced tomatoes
6 cups Fish Stock (page 10)
1 teaspoon salt
$1/2$ teaspoon freshly ground black pepper
$1/2$ teaspoon dried thyme
$1/2$ teaspoon dried basil
$1/2$ teaspoon dried oregano
1 teaspoon Cajun or Old Bay seasoning
1 bay leaf
$1/2$ teaspoon cayenne pepper
1 teaspoon Tabasco
$1^1/2$ pounds smoked Andouille sausage or kielbasa
$1/2$ pound okra, cut into pieces
1 pound shrimp, peeled and deveined
1 pound claw or lump crab-meat, fresh or pasteurized (page 108)
Cooked white rice for serving

Put the crayfish in a deep pot and rinse quickly in two or three changes of cold water. Drain and set aside. The pot should be deep enough to keep the crayfish from escaping.

Heat the oil in a heavy-bottomed stock pot until smoking hot. Whisk in the flour and stir constantly over medium-high heat until the mixture turns a dark reddish brown, 3 to 6 minutes. Keep whisking the roux or it will burn and stick to the bottom. Be careful not to splash it on your skin.

When the roux is properly browned, turn off the heat and stir in the onion, celery, bell pepper, green onions, and garlic. Return to medium heat and cook, stirring constantly, until the vegetables are soft and browned, 6 to 8 minutes.

Add the tomatoes, stock, salt, black pepper, thyme, basil, oregano, Cajun seasoning, bay leaf, cayenne, and Tabasco. Add whole pieces of sausage. Bring to a boil, reduce the heat, and simmer, uncovered, for 1 hour. Remove the whole sausage and cut into $1/4$-inch slices and return to pot. *(continued)*

Stir in the okra and simmer for 30 minutes more. Add the crayfish to the pot, along with the shrimp, and bring almost to a boil. Cook for 5 minutes. Add the crabmeat and cook for 10 minutes more. Remove from the heat and let sit for at least an hour to let the flavors blend. Reheat and serve over white rice.

NOTE: You can substitute 1 pound of frozen, cooked crayfish for fresh, but do not add them until you add the crabmeat.

Gulf Coast Texas is known not just for its variety of fresh seafood, but also for Texas beef. Cattle ranches sprang up early in Texas, and port cities such as Galveston and Corpus Christi were important to the business, both for importing and exporting cattle and meat.

Texas Cowboy Chili Stew

King Ranch, outside Corpus Christi, known as the birthplace of American ranching, is larger than the state of Rhode Island. Ranching and cowboys still conjure visions of chuck wagons, open fires, and large pots of stews simmering on the starlit range. Texans love their chili, and this recipe blends a number of traditions—the cattle ranch, the hot-as-Hades-spiciness locals love, and the Hispanic influence of corn, both in the hominy and masa harina. I like to serve this chili with South of the Mason-Dixon Line Cornbread (page 230).

Serves 6 to 8

6 tablespoons vegetable oil
2 pounds lean beef, cut into
    1-inch pieces
1 onion, chopped
$^1/_2$ cup diced celery
$^1/_2$ cup diced carrots
2 tablespoons minced garlic
$^1/_2$ cup masa harina (see note)
    or flour
6 cups beef stock or bouillon
3 large tomatoes, peeled,
    seeded, and chopped, or
    one 28-ounce can diced
    tomatoes, drained
2 tablespoons tomato paste
1 teaspoon oregano
2 teaspoons ground cumin
2 tomatillos, peeled, cored,
    and finely chopped
2 to 4 hot chiles, such as
    serrano or jalapeño,
    chopped (see note)
2 teaspoons chipotle chile
    powder, or other ground
    red pepper
2 teaspoons salt
One 14-ounce can hominy,
    broken apart and rinsed
One 14-ounce can pinto or
    red beans, drained
Salt and freshly ground black
    pepper

Heat the oil in a Dutch oven and brown the beef well on all sides. Place the beef on a plate and set aside.

Add the onion, celery, carrots, and garlic and sauté for about 5 minutes. Add the masa harina and stir constantly for about 3 minutes, taking care not to let it brown. Stir in the beef stock or bouillon slowly, taking care not to allow lumps to form. Add the tomatoes, tomato paste, oregano, cumin, tomatillos, chiles, chipotle chile powder, and salt.

Return the beef to the pot and stir. Bring stew to a boil, reduce heat, cover, and allow to simmer for about 1 hour and 15 minutes. Check the beef to see if it is tender; if not, continue cooking for another 10 to 15 minutes.

Add the hominy and beans and stir, cover, and simmer for 15 minutes longer. Remove from heat and let sit for at least 1 hour before serving. Briefly reheat and add salt and pepper to taste.

NOTE: Masa harina, tortilla dough flour, is available at Latin markets. Wear gloves when handling chiles and do not touch bare skin.

The Tillamook County Creamery Association is a nearly one-hundred-year-old farmer-owned co-op situated on Tillamook Bay on the rugged Oregon coast that produces some of the finest cheese in America. Making my way to the creamery meant going through miles and miles of ancient moss-encrusted trees that finally gave way to the lush green farmlands of Tillamook. The Tillamook sharp cheddar recipe is as old as the creamery, and has been fashioned here into a hearty cheesy brew by Billy Hahn, chef of Jake's Famous Crawfish Restaurant in Portland.

Tillamook Cheddar Cheese and Lager Soup

Serves 4

4 tablespoons ($^1/_2$ stick) butter
4 tablespoons all-purpose flour
3 cups milk
1 tablespoon minced garlic
Salt and freshly ground black pepper
$^1/_2$ teaspoon crushed red chiles, chopped
2 cups extra-sharp cheddar cheese, shredded
$^3/_4$ cup dark beer

Heat the butter in a sauté pan. Add the flour and cook on low heat. Stir mixture until it starts to bubble. Do not allow it to brown. Remove from heat and set aside.

Heat the milk in a saucepan until it is just about to boil. Add the garlic, salt and pepper to taste, and crushed chiles. Stir this mixture until just before boiling.

Add half of the butter-flour mixture and stir with a wire whisk until it reaches a low simmer. Add more butter-flour mixture as needed to thicken. Stir constantly to avoid burning.

Turn down the heat and add the cheese and beer, stirring to allow the cheese to melt. The soup should have a smooth, consistent texture. It may be reheated at a low temperature. (Do not boil.)

TILLAMOOK COUNTY, OREGON

Tillamook County, Oregon, home to about 24,000 people and slightly more cows, has long been a major dairy-farming area. Today it's notable as the home of the 150-member Tillamook County Creamery Association, which since 1909 has been turning out quality cheddar cheese and other dairy products. The co-op produces nearly one-third of all the milk in Oregon and, besides its commercial operations, sponsors education and literacy programs and plays host to a million visitors a year, some of whom probably arrive thinking that milk comes from refrigerators. Tillamook makes eight varieties of cheddar cheese, including Vintage White Extra Sharp Smoked, as well as Monterey Jack and Colby cheeses. It also offers ice cream, butter, and sour cream. Cows probably aren't affected by scenery, but the ninety inches of average precipitation per year must make the grass near Oregon's coast pretty tasty.

In Rockport, Texas, the ever-popular AransaZu restaurant serves up some of the Texas Gulf Coast's most creative fare. Here chef-owner Jay Moore prepares a creamy, sherry-enhanced artichoke soup that may be easily turned into a crab-and-artichoke version with the addition of lightly sautéed mushrooms and Gulf lump crabmeat. This soup made with fresh artichoke hearts is an amazing culinary experience— if fresh artichokes are available and if you have the time to trim and prepare them.

Rockport Artichoke Soup

Serves 4 to 6

3 tablespoons olive oil
2 tablespoons minced garlic
4 tablespoons minced red
  onion
1 bottle (750 milliliters) dry
  sherry
3 cups (two 14-ounce cans)
  artichoke hearts, drained
  and quartered
3 cups Chicken or Vegetable
  Stock (recipes follow)
1 cup heavy cream
3 tablespoons cornstarch
Salt and white pepper
1 cup sliced mushrooms,
  sautéed in olive oil or
  butter, for garnish,
  optional
1 teaspoon fresh or dried
  tarragon, for garnish,
  optional
$^{1}/_{2}$ to 1 pound sautéed lump
  crabmeat (amount
  depends on how "crabby"
  you want the soup to be),
  for garnish, optional

In a saucepan, heat olive oil over medium heat. Add the garlic and onion and sauté until onion is translucent. Remove and reserve garlic-onion mixture. Deglaze the pan with 1 cup of sherry, reducing by half.

Marinate the drained artichoke hearts in 1 cup sherry for 20 minutes.

Return the garlic-onion mixture to the saucepan and add the stock. Bring to a boil. Reduce to a simmer and cook for 20 minutes.

Strain the sherry from the artichokes, reserving artichokes, and add the strained sherry and heavy cream to the stock mixture. Bring to a boil. Mix the cornstarch with 3 tablespoons of water to form a light paste and, off the heat, add to the stock mixture. Whisk the soup mixture well and return to medium heat for 15 minutes.

Season to taste with salt and white pepper. Fold in the artichoke hearts. Add more sherry if desired. Taste and adjust seasonings. Add garnishes, if using, and serve immediately.

Chicken Stock

Makes about 2½ quarts

One 3-pound chicken, cut
    into pieces
2 medium onions, sliced
4 celery stalks, chopped
2 carrots, chopped
4 whole garlic cloves,
    unpeeled
2 bay leaves
2 teaspoons dried thyme
6 sprigs parsley

Rinse the chicken parts well in cold water. Combine chicken and all the other ingredients in a large stock pot, add 12 cups of water, and bring to a boil. Simmer, uncovered, for 2 to 2½ hours, skimming off surface foam frequently. Strain the stock through a fine sieve or cheesecloth. Chill and degrease. Stock that will not be used within 3 to 4 days may be frozen.

Vegetable Stock

Makes about 1½ quarts

2 tablespoons olive oil
2 onions, peeled and sliced
2 carrots, coarsely chopped
4 celery stalks, coarsely
    chopped (include a little of
    the leafy tops)
1 bunch green onions,
    chopped
6 whole garlic cloves,
    unpeeled and smashed
1 teaspoon whole black
    peppercorns
½ bunch parsley (about 6
    sprigs)
3 bay leaves
1 tablespoon salt, or to taste

Heat the olive oil in a stock pot and add the onions, carrots, celery, green onions, and garlic. Sauté over medium heat for about 5 minutes, stirring often. Add the remaining ingredients and 2 quarts of cold water, and bring to a boil. Reduce heat and continue to cook, uncovered, for 30 minutes. Remove stock from the heat and let it sit for 20 minutes before straining.

NOTES: This is a basic vegetable stock and the ingredients may be adjusted, depending on what it will be used with or on the time of the year. In the summer, you may want to add some tomato and squash, and in the winter, leeks, mushrooms, and a little celery root. To make a darker "brown stock," continue sautéing the vegetables for about 15 minutes, to brown them first, then add the flavorings, 2 tablespoons tomato paste, and the water.

This stock can be made 2 to 3 days ahead or, if you want to stay ahead of the game, freeze a batch in ice cube trays and store the frozen cubes in a plastic freezer bag—it keeps for several months.

I began my cooking career on the Cape, where I fell in love with this soup. This is my rendition of the one I first sampled at the legendary Moors Restaurant. This family restaurant on the very tip of the Cape, in Provincetown, Massachusetts, is a culinary institution famous for its Portuguese fare. The actual name of this rich stew in Portuguese is couvres, and it is a deceptively simple dish. With the flavor of the perfectly spiced chorizo sausage permeating the pot of beans and kale, the resulting soup is nothing short of marvelous. I have enjoyed many meals of this soup with a simple salad of local greens and a generous portion of crusty Portuguese bread.

Cape Cod Portuguese Kale Soup

Serves 6 to 8

1 cup small white beans
3 tablespoons olive oil
1 large onion, diced
1 tablespoon chopped garlic
12 cups Chicken or Vegetable
    Stock (page 35)
1 pound chorizo sausage or
    spicy kielbasa, cut into
    ¼-inch slices
1 pound kale, washed,
    stemmed, and coarsely
    chopped
1 tablespoon salt
Freshly ground black pepper
2 tablespoons red wine
    vinegar, or more to taste
3 cups cubed potatoes

Soak beans overnight in cold water. Drain and set beans aside.

In a heavy-bottomed stock pot, heat the olive oil and sauté the onion for 3 minutes over medium heat. Add the chopped garlic and sauté for 1 minute more. Add the beans and the chicken stock. Bring to a boil and reduce heat. Add the chorizo and cook gently for 1 hour. Add the kale, salt, pepper to taste, vinegar, and cubed potatoes. Continue cooking for 1 hour more, stirring often. Adjust the seasonings and serve with crusty bread and sweet butter. This soup is even better when made a day ahead.

PROVINCETOWN, MASSACHUSETTS

Provincetown, Massachusetts, on the inside of the very tiptop of the spiral of land that forms Cape Cod, manages to combine individuality with community, hardworking fishermen with high-living revelers, and history with "edge." It was the first stop for the *Mayflower,* pausing on its way across Cape Cod Bay to Plymouth, and it's the must-stop for hundreds of thousands of vacationers, who enjoy its myriad restaurants, boutiques, and art galleries. In the 1920s, artists and writers began flocking here, attracted by the beautiful scenery and the clear island light. In the 1960s, the laid-back lifestyle began attracting a flourishing gay community. The town is big enough to be host to the Great Schooner Regatta every fall (won in 2003 by our very own *Pride of Baltimore II,* with skipper Jan Miles), and small enough to embrace an annual Pet Awareness Week, with games, a Doggy Kiss-Off, and a Pet Drag Tea Party. It's a place where you can watch artists paint, whales breach, and leaves turn brilliant in the fall. You can dine on boiled lobster (see Lobster 101, page 140), Steamed Clams (page 143), or Cape Cod Portuguese Kale Soup (page 36). Haute or humble, P'town has something for everybody.

Daisy Barquest, a native of Jacksonville, Florida (which she says is really southern Georgia), likes to tell friends about the wonders of boiled peanuts (see sidebar), which are to be found on nearly every back road in northern Florida and southern Georgia. The residents of the southern Atlantic region do indeed have a culinary love affair with peanuts, and this Deep South medley of ingredients is a fantastic, almost bisquelike soup. One of the wonderful aspects of this soup is that it can be served hot or cold. If one has the time, boiled peanuts removed from the shell and skinned could be pureed and used in place of the peanut butter.

Daisy's Jacksonville Peanut Soup

Serves 6

3 tablespoons butter
1 small onion, finely chopped
3 green onions, minced
2 garlic cloves, minced
2 serrano chiles, finely chopped (see note)
2 tablespoons all-purpose flour
2 cups Chicken Stock (page 35)
4 tablespoons honey
2 cups milk
2 cups coconut milk
2 cups peanut butter (chunky is good, but smooth will work, too)
Salt and freshly ground black pepper
$1/2$ cup whipping cream
6 tablespoon roasted peanuts, coarsely chopped

In a stock pot, melt the butter and sauté the onion, green onions, garlic, and chiles over low heat for 5 minutes. Whisk in the flour and stir constantly for 3 minutes. Off the heat, whisk in the chicken stock and 2 tablespoons of the honey, return to the stove, and bring to a boil. Reduce heat and add the milk, coconut milk, and peanut butter. Season to taste with salt and pepper. Simmer gently, stirring often, for about 15 minutes.

Pour the whipping cream into a chilled mixing bowl and whisk in the remaining 2 tablespoons honey. Whip the cream until soft peaks form. Do not over whip. Ladle the soup into bowls and garnish with a dollop of cream and a sprinkle of roasted peanuts.

NOTE: Wear gloves when handling chiles and don't touch bare skin.

PEANUTS—RAW, DRY ROASTED, SALTED, OR . . . BOILED?   Peanuts have always been big business in this country. Fortunes have been made or lost in the growing and selling of them. Ballgames just wouldn't be ballgames without them. One of our presidents even farmed them. Most of us have enjoyed our peanuts whirled into peanut butter or as slabs of peanut brittle. But down in Jacksonville, Florida, and southern Georgia, there is an ancient tradition still taking place that many of us are not even aware of. But thanks to Daisy Barquest, formerly of Jacksonville, it will now see the light of day. According to Daisy, her dad was a military officer, and in summers they made their way from Jacksonville to the barracks at Camp Blanding, which it turns out was a much-anticipated annual trip.

"As soon as you ventured out of Jacksonville a little inland, there were big kettles over open fires on the side of the roads with hand-painted signs on pieces of wood, leaning up against a barrel or bucket, proclaiming 'Boiled Peanuts.' We got so excited just thinking about the boiled peanuts. We would stop and get a sack. You pop them in your mouth and they are all salty and soft. The trick was you couldn't use your hands to peel them. You would first suck out all the salty water and then, with your tongue, smash the shell of the peanut against the roof of your mouth, wiggling it around, until you get the shell to slide off the nut. Then you threw out the shell and ate the nut."

Daisy and her siblings were crazy for the boiled peanuts and coerced their mom into making them at home, a practice that, according to Daisy, did not last long. "My mom said she didn't want to make them at home anymore because they took all day to cook, about six to seven hours, and as soon as she had put them into the big soup pot and brought them to a boil, us kids would keep asking . . . every few minutes . . . if they were done yet. It drove her mad and she said, 'No more boiled peanuts at home.'" To this day, Daisy will, from time to time, percolate herself a batch if she runs into some raw peanuts at her local farmers market. She says that when she visits northern Florida now you can find the boiled nuts in the cities, at produce stores, sold as salted, or Cajun-style. She doesn't fancy these peanuts too much because "you need to see the person who cooked the nuts face-to-face, to know if they're going to be good."

You need raw peanuts to make the proper boiled peanut, along with a pot with ample room for the nuts and for water to generously cover them. First, you wash the nuts in cold water and then place them in the pot. Cover with cold water and pour salt . . . lots of salt . . . into the water. Bring the whole pot to a boil, reduce the heat a little, and continue cooking for five to seven hours, adding more water if too much cooks off. Daisy found cooking the peanuts inside made the house too hot, so she cooks them outside over a grill now. The way you know if the peanuts are finished is the official taste test. The nut (not the shell) should be "totally soft, absolutely no crunch to it, sort of like over-cooked veggies, or the best description would be 'a way overdone lima bean.'" They are best eaten warm, but if you have any left over (which, if you have a crowd around, you probably won't), put them in the fridge and they'll keep for a couple of days.

Most times when you see a recipe for potato leek–style soup, you think of a thick soup. But this creation from chef Greg Higgins of Portland, Oregon, is an unusually light, seafood-scented soup accented with a touch of saffron and bits of delicately smoked salmon floated in just before serving.

Higgins's Saffron Potato-Leek Soup

Serves 8

$1/4$ cup olive oil

1 onion, diced

2 large leeks, white part plus 2 inches of the green, diced (see note)

3 garlic cloves, peeled and coarsely chopped

1 small pinch saffron

1 cup white wine

1 to 2 large Yukon Gold potatoes, diced

6 cups Fish Stock (page 10)

$3/4$ cup half-and-half

2 bay leaves

$1/3$ pound smoked salmon, flaked, for garnish

2 tablespoons chopped fresh chives, for garnish

Heat the olive oil over medium heat in a large heavy-bottomed saucepan or stock pot. Add the onion, leeks, garlic, and saffron and sauté until the onion and leeks are translucent, about 10 minutes. Add the wine, diced potatoes, fish stock, half-and-half, and bay leaves. Bring liquid up to a simmer, stirring frequently to avoid any scorching. Cook over medium heat for 30 minutes. Remove from heat and cool. Puree cooled mixture, in batches, in a blender, then strain through a fine-mesh strainer. Reheat as necessary and garnish with smoked salmon and chives.

NOTE: Leeks are notorious for containing loads of sand. They need to be quartered lengthwise and washed several times in cold water before dicing.

Steven Raichlen, cookbook author, cooking teacher, food writer, and lecturer, is one of south Florida's most inventive cooks, as this recipe, adapted from his book Miami Spice: The New Florida Cuisine, *well demonstrates. Steve explains that he developed this recipe because someone gave him a stovetop smoker as a present, but he also has devised a clever way to do stovetop smoking in a large wok with a tight-fitting lid and a round cake rack. As he describes it, you line the wok with aluminum foil, place a few hardwood smoking chips in the bottom, position the cake rack above the chips, and place the vegetables on the rack. Turn your stove's exhaust fan on high, and put the wok on a burner over high heat. When the chips start to smoke, cover the wok tightly and lower heat to medium. And, oh yes, one more thing: Steve warns that you may have to disable your smoke alarm temporarily.*

Steve's Smoked Gazpacho

Serves 4

4 large ripe tomatoes, halved
1 yellow bell pepper, halved, cored, and seeded
1 red bell pepper, halved, cored, and seeded
2 cucumbers, peeled, halved, and seeded
1 onion, halved
4 garlic cloves
4 green onions
4 to 5 tablespoons extra virgin olive oil
4 to 5 tablespoons red wine vinegar
$^1/_2$ cup chopped fresh herbs, such as basil, parsley, and oregano or thyme
$^1/_8$ teaspoon cayenne pepper, or to taste
Salt and freshly ground black pepper
Juice of $^1/_2$ lime
1 ripe avocado, peeled and chopped, for garnish
3 tablespoons chopped fresh chives or green onions, for garnish

Put the tomatoes, bell peppers, cucumbers, onion, garlic, and green onions in a smoker, cut side up. Place the smoker over high heat until wisps of smoke appear. Then cover tightly, reduce the heat to medium, and smoke vegetables for 20 to 30 minutes, until hot and soft. Let cool.

Place the smoked vegetables, oil, vinegar, herbs, cayenne, and salt and pepper to taste in a blender or food processor and blend at high speed or process until smooth. Taste and adjust seasonings. Chill the soup in a covered container. Before serving, stir in the lime juice and garnish with avocado and chives.

My friend the late Maggie Haines, formerly of Cecil County on the Eastern Shore of the Chesapeake Bay, made this soup every summer when the melons are at their sweetest. When Maggie originally gave me the recipe, she pulled me aside to tell me, "Don't eat the soup too fast, or you'll get dizzy."

Maggie's Eastern Shore Cantaloupe Soup

We prepare this soup often in the warm months at my restaurant and drizzle a little fresh berry puree on top just before serving. This recipe also works beautifully with other ripe melons, such as honeydew.

Serves 6 to 8

4 ripe cantaloupes
One 750-milliliter bottle dry champagne
1/2 cup freshly chopped mint
Mint sprigs, for garnish
Fresh Berry Sauce, optional (recipe follows)

Peel and seed 3 of the cantaloupes and cut into pieces. Puree the cantaloupe in a blender in batches, adding champagne to each batch to create a thickish soup consistency. Chill well.

Cut the remaining melon in half, discard the seeds, and scoop out the flesh with a melon baller. Add these balls to the chilled pureed melon, along with the chopped mint. Serve in chilled bowls with a mint sprig.

Fresh Berry Sauce

2 pints fresh raspberries or strawberries
1/2 cup sugar dissolved in 1/2 cup hot water
2 tablespoons freshly squeezed lemon juice

Puree berries in a blender. With the blender running, pour in the sugar water and the lemon juice and process until smooth. Put the puree through a sieve, if necessary, to remove the seeds. Refrigerated sauce will keep for several days.

Coastal-style cooking involves countless varieties of seafood and shellfish. Think of cod, scrod, sole, floun- der, bluefish, rockfish, redfish, swordfish, whitefish, monkfish, pompano, trout, shad, grouper, perch, catfish, black bass, red snapper, sea trout, pollack, haddock, her- ring, halibut, sturgeon, salmon, and tuna—just to name a few. Some fish are unique to a region, while others can be found in a number of different areas. For example, cod is normally only found in the North Atlantic waters of New England, while salmon is found on both coasts, in salt and fresh water—yet each region has its own meth- ods of cooking. Seafood can be prepared in endless ways—baked or poached, grilled or roasted, steamed or fried.

3 FISH

Coastal dwellers have long had an advantage over in- land folks when it comes to seafood, and while there's still some advantage in terms of variety, technology has made it much easier to preserve and transport delicate fish and seafood. Now even if you don't live in a coastal region, you can enjoy fresh fish of all kinds. Fish has become more popular than ever in the past decade or so, when the health benefits of a fish-filled diet became clear. Not only is fish rich in vitamins—A, B, D, and E—it also has essential minerals—iron, iodine, zinc, selenium, copper, and cobalt, among others. But there's another compound in fish that makes it spectacularly healthy, and that's the essential omega-3 fatty acids, which are particularly prevalent in cold-water fish. Omega-3s are a form of polyunsaturated fat that the body needs but can't produce. Consumption of omega-3 fatty acids is said to ward off illnesses such as hypertension and diabetes and to improve immune defenses and lessen the risk of stroke. There's also evidence that omega-3s improve brain function and may even reduce the risks of some kinds of cancers. The American Heart Association recommends eating fish, particularly fatty fish such as salmon, tuna, and mackerel, at least twice a week. Having said all that, however, there's really only one compelling reason to eat seafood: It's absolutely delicious.

My good friend Cesar Calderon and I met years ago in northern California, where he was a well-known seafood chef. He has always been rooted in Pacific seafood cooking, only his roots are from farther south—in Mexico, to be exact. I have had the pleasure of sampling hundreds of the señor's seafood creations, and his Acapulco-style ceviche is one of my favorites. Ceviche (also spelled "cebiche" and "seviche") is normally made from a flatfish such as flounder or halibut, but also works nicely with red snapper. People often refer to ceviche as a "raw fish" dish, but actually the acid in the citrus "cooks" the fish. Cesar suggests an alternative method of serving would be to place the finished ceviche into an attractive serving bowl, topping with the final third of the Salsa Fresca, and garnishing with avocado and cilantro. Tortilla chips could be served on the side, allowing guests to scoop up the ceviche with the chips. For a completely different ceviche experience, after "cooking" in the lime juice, use a similar volume of the Big Bowl Zesty Tropical Salsa (page 223) in place of the Salsa Fresca.

Señor Calderon's Ceviche

Serves 6

1 pound flounder, sole, or halibut fillet
Juice of 7 to 8 large limes (about 1 1/2 cups)
Salsa Fresca (recipe follows)
1 medium avocado, peeled and sliced, for garnish
Whole sprigs of cilantro, for garnish

Cut the fillets into 3/4-inch pieces and toss with lime juice in a mixing bowl. Cover and place in the refrigerator and let the fish "cook" in the lime juice for at least 6 to 8 hours, or overnight. Stir the fish from time to time.

About one hour before serving, add two-thirds of the Salsa Fresca to the fish and fold together. Return to the refrigerator for at least one hour, as the mixture should be very cold when served. To serve, mound ceviche mixture into cocktail glasses (martini glasses work well) and top with the remaining Salsa Fresca. Garnish the glasses with slices of avocado and sprigs of cilantro. Serve at once.

Salsa Fresca

3 ripe, medium-sized
    tomatoes, cored, seeded,
    and chopped
3 to 4 serrano chiles, or to
    taste, finely chopped (see
    note)
1/4 cup olive oil
1/2 teaspoon chopped fresh
    oregano (dried will work
    as well)
1 small red onion, finely
    diced
1 teaspoon salt
Freshly ground black pepper
4 tablespoons chopped fresh
    cilantro

In a mixing bowl, combine the tomatoes, chiles, olive oil, oregano, red onion, salt, pepper to taste, and chopped cilantro. Mix together well and refrigerate for 2 to 3 hours.

NOTE: Wear gloves when handling chiles and do not touch bare skin.

When this Chesapeake Bay boy first moved to California, his seafood knowledge was limited to the basic East Coast preparations he had grown up with. The San Francisco Bay area was a culinary awakening for me, with ingredients and cooking techniques that were totally new and mysterious. I landed in a small French restaurant, A La Carte, owned by chef Annette Esser, who introduced me to my first mousse.

Sole and Smoked Salmon Mousse with Dill Shallot Butter Sauce

Serves 6

1$\frac{1}{4}$ pounds sole fillets, cut into small pieces

$\frac{1}{4}$ pound smoked salmon (or other smoked fish, such as trout or sturgeon)

Pinch of kosher salt

2 tablespoons fresh lemon juice

3 egg whites

1 cup heavy cream

Dill Shallot Butter Sauce (recipe follows)

I, like many other people I know, thought of mousse only as a dessert—in fact, up to that time, the closest thing to a mousse I had experienced was a package of Whip 'n Chill. Annette was a marvel with seafood mousse; her sea scallop version was so light and airy you needed a sauce to hold it on the plate.

This rendition pairs sole (which sounds nice, but in this country is really flounder) and lightly smoked salmon. The mousse may be served as an entrée or, baked in individual ramekins, as a first course. The mixture is quite versatile, allowing for other fish substitutions. By baking the mixture in a small, thin loaf pan, and then chilling well after baking, it can be turned out onto a platter and served as a fish mousse pâté with water crackers or baguette rounds.

Place the work bowl and metal blade of a food processor in the refrigerator to chill before making the mousse.

Place the sole fillets, smoked salmon, salt, and lemon juice into the chilled work bowl and process until quite smooth. Add the egg whites and continue to process until silky smooth. Use a rubber spatula to scrape down the edges of the work bowl to make sure all the mixture is incorporated, and process briefly again.

With the processor running, slowly add the cream, stopping the processor a couple of times to scrape down the sides, until all the cream is blended in. This mixture can be made ahead and refrigerated until ready to cook. *(continued)*

Preheat the oven to 325°F.

Butter six 3-inch ceramic ramekins and evenly divide the mixture among them. Place the ramekins in a pan that will be able to accommodate a water bath and pour boiling water into the pan until the water comes about halfway up the sides of the ramekins. Bake for 35 or 40 minutes, or until a thin knife inserted in the center comes out clean. After baking, remove the ramekins from the water and let rest for 10 minutes before serving.

Invert each ramekin onto a small serving plate and lightly drizzle the mousse with desired sauce, such as the Dill Shallot Butter below or a hollandaise-based sauce.

Dill Shallot Butter Sauce

Makes about 1 cup
1 cup dry white wine
$1/4$ cup white wine vinegar or champagne vinegar
2 tablespoons minced shallots
$1/4$ cup heavy whipping cream
$1/2$ pound (2 sticks) unsalted butter, cut into small pieces
Pinch of salt
$1/4$ cup finely chopped fresh dill

Place the wine, vinegar, and shallots in a saucepan, and cook over medium heat until the volume is reduced by half, about 5 minutes. Add the whipping cream and continue to cook until volume is reduced to about 4 tablespoons.

Remove saucepan from the heat and whisk in the butter pieces, a little bit at a time. Season with salt to taste and add the chopped dill and stir well. Hold in a warm spot, but not over direct heat, until ready to use.

Beginning with the Native Americans, seafood from the Chesapeake Bay has been fashioned into all sorts of cakes, pies, skewers, and fritters. These little delectables have long been a favorite here in Baltimore, at municipal markets, carts on the side of the road, and drugstore soda fountains. They are not cod cakes, which are made from fresh cod. Coddies are made from shredded salt cod that has been first soaked in water. Baltimore culinary protocol requires that coddies be eaten on saltine crackers with mustard. We generally do not use fancy mustard—a simple deli-style is just the ticket. Great served as a light meal, with a green salad, or as an appetizer.

Lexington Market Coddies

Makes 18 to 20

1 pound dried salted codfish
1 1/2 pounds white potatoes, peeled and cut into quarters
2 tablespoons vegetable oil or melted butter
1 small onion, finely diced
3 eggs, beaten
4 tablespoons minced chives
1/3 cup finely chopped parsley
Salt and freshly ground black pepper
Oil for frying
Saltine crackers, for serving
Mustard, for serving

Soak the codfish in a bowl of cold water for 24 hours, changing the water approximately every 6 hours. When ready to prepare the recipe, place the codfish in a saucepan. Cover with water, bring to a boil, reduce the heat, and simmer for 15 minutes. Drain and break up the fish into flakes with a fork. Cool.

Cook the potatoes in lightly salted water until tender, then drain and mash well. Let the potatoes cool.

Heat the oil or butter in a sauté pan and gently sauté the onion for 5 minutes, taking care not to let it brown.

Place the codfish and potatoes in a bowl and mix together with the additional ingredients. Form the coddies into small balls and flatten to about 1/2-inch thick.

Pour oil into a heavy skillet to a depth of about 1 1/2 inches. Heat the oil and fry the coddies, a few at a time, until golden brown, about 3 minutes on each side. Remove with a slotted spoon to paper towels to drain.

The coddies can be served hot, warm, or at room temperature. Serve on crackers with mustard on the side.

I lived for many years in the San Francisco Bay area, and one of my favorite day trips was wandering around the Mission Street district. Once home to San Francisco's Irish working class, it has been transformed into a bustling Hispanic neighborhood. Cantinas, restaurants, outdoor markets, and taquerias line the palm-shaded boulevard, offering sights, sounds, and aromas that vicariously transport visitors to Central and South America. Toward the end of the day, my ritual was to treat myself to a fish taco, with firm-fleshed fish, fresh from the grill, wrapped in a small, warm flour tortilla, topped with an array of fresh ingredients. Sometimes the fish taquitos are served in fried corn tortilla shells in place of the fresh flour variety. Try both to see what suits your taste.

Mission Street Fish Taquitos

Serves 4

1 pound mahi mahi, rockfish, or snapper fillets

$1/4$ cup olive oil

3 tablespoons fresh lime juice

$1/2$ teaspoon minced garlic

1 small serrano chile, seeded and minced (see note)

1 teaspoon ancho chile powder

2 tablespoons finely chopped cilantro

8 soft flour tortillas (taco size)

Cilantro Cream (recipe follows)

Salsa Fresca (see page 47)

Shredded lettuce

Diced red onion

Finely sliced green onion

Chopped cilantro

Hot sauce

Place the fish in a glass baking dish. In a small bowl, mix the olive oil, lime juice, garlic, serrano chile, chile powder, and cilantro. Pour evenly over the fish fillets and turn the fish several times to coat. Cover and place in the refrigerator for 30 minutes, turning once during that time. While the fish is marinating, assemble the serving ingredients and preheat the grill. Remove the fish from the marinade and place on the hot grill, skin side up. Cook for about $2^{1}/2$ to 3 minutes per side, depending on the thickness of the fillet. Place the cooked fillets on a platter and let stand for 2 minutes. While the fish is resting, warm the tortillas on the grill. Cut or flake the fish into pieces to fit inside the tortillas.

To assemble, place fish, a dab of Cilantro Cream, a tablespoonful of Salsa Fresca, and any or all of the other accompaniments desired in each tortilla. Serve at once. Cuban-Style Black Beans (page 211) on the side make a perfect combo.

NOTE: Wear gloves when handling chiles and do not touch bare skin.

Cilantro Cream

^{2}/3 cup sour cream
^{1}/4 cup mayonnaise
1 teaspoon minced garlic
Juice of 1 lime
^{1}/4 cup minced cilantro

Mix all the ingredients well in a bowl.

CHILES   As recently as fifteen or twenty years ago, the hottest spices most Americans ever tasted were black pepper, yellow mustard, and, occasionally, horseradish. But a booming economy and a burgeoning population of immigrants from Latin America and the Far East fostered a culinary revolution. Suddenly, salt and pepper were passé; peppers were in. Ten years ago, the only hot peppers you could find in supermarkets came in a can, sliced or chopped; today even my neighborhood grocery stores stock fresh jalapeños, serranos, and even the fiery Scotch bonnets in their produce sections. Japanese wasabi and Chinese horseradish are readily available, too, and there are whole stores devoted to hot sauces, literally thousands of them, with names like "Angel of Death" and "Texas Fire Water." The heat is on!

Chef Su-Mei Yu, the first lady of Thai cooking, holds court in her popular restaurant, Saffron—a terrific casual Thai noodle restaurant and rotisserie chicken takeout shop in San Diego. She was raised in Bangkok and often returns to her homeland to teach cook-

New Year Noodles with Fish Curry Sauce

ing classes to ensure that as Asia becomes more developed, the cuisine she loves so well continues to be passed down to the next generation, as has been the case for countless preceding generations. "The lesson I learned is that food is what connects you to who you are, and who your ancestors were." She adds that "Thai food is not just good food, it is homeopathic, and keeps one in harmony."

As you will be able to taste in this delightful fish curry, Su-Mei loves seafood. One of her friends does tuna farming in Ensenada and she invites him and other like-minded cooking buddies to "tuna parties," where everyone pitches in and cooks up a feast of fresh tuna and other straight-from-the ocean delicacies. Su-Mei's first cookbook, Cracking the Coconut: Classic Thai Home Cooking, *won an IACP award for the best book by a first-time author.*

Serves 6

1 cup yogurt
1/4 cup chopped onion
1 garlic clove, minced
2 teaspoons lemon juice
1 teaspoon ground coriander
1 teaspoon cayenne pepper
1 teaspoon ground ginger
1 teaspoon oregano
1/2 teaspoon turmeric
1/4 teaspoon curry powder
1/2 cup extra virgin olive oil
1/8 teaspoon cumin seed
4 whitefish or flounder fillets
1 pound dried vermicelli

Preheat the oven to 350°F.

Put all the ingredients except the fish fillets, oil, cumin seed, and vermicelli into the bowl of a food processor fitted with the metal blade and blend until thoroughly mixed. Cut the fish fillets into halves and arrange in a shallow baking dish.

Combine the oil and cumin seed in a skillet and heat until cumin is dark brown. Add the blended ingredients, stirring constantly. Pour the mixture over the fish and bake for 10 to 15 minutes, until the fish is cooked through but still moist and flaky.

Prepare the vermicelli according to package directions. Drain. To serve, divide noodles evenly among plates and top with sauce.

Seafood lovers tend to do a lot of stuffing. We stuff shrimp, calamari, whole fish, clams, and the easiest of all—fish fillets. This style of stuffing is indicative of recipes from the Mid-Atlantic, the Carolinas, and Louisiana. Most stuffing will have a primary base of breading or breadcrumbs with added seafood, vegetables, and seasonings. I am disposed to the style of stuffing that is mostly seafood, with just a little filler or breading added to hold it together. Improvisation works well with stuffing. Just change the types of seafood or seasoning to suit your taste. Given the origins of this recipe, a good bet for a side will always be rice—plain or fancy. I have provided a Simple Lemon Butter recipe for this dish, but Dill Shallot Butter Sauce (page 50) is also terrific.

Another variation is to forget the fish fillets and double the ingredients for the stuffing—you now have a genuine Seafood Imperial. Bake in a casserole or mound the mixture into individual shell-shaped baking dishes (available at most cookware stores). The baking time will be the same for the casserole, and a little less time if baked in shells.

Sole with Seafood Imperial

Serves 6

4 tablespoons ($^1/_2$ stick) butter or olive oil

$^1/_4$ cup green bell pepper, diced

$^1/_4$ cup red or yellow bell pepper, diced

$^1/_2$ cup mayonnaise

$^1/_2$ teaspoon Dijon mustard

1 teaspoon seafood or Cajun seasoning

Freshly ground black pepper

2 lemons

2 tablespoons chopped parsley

$^1/_2$ pound lump crabmeat, picked over for shells

$^1/_2$ pound steamed or boiled shrimp, peeled, deveined, and chopped

$^1/_4$ pound broiled or sautéed scallops, diced

Six 6-ounce sole or flounder fillets

Salt and pepper, for seasoning

$1^1/_2$ cups dry white wine, heated to the boiling point

Simple Lemon Butter (recipe follows)

Preheat the oven to 375°F.

Melt 2 tablespoons of the butter in a sauté pan over medium heat and sauté the bell peppers until soft.

In a small mixing bowl, combine the mayonnaise, mustard, seafood seasoning, pepper to taste, the juice of 1 lemon, and the parsley.

Place the crabmeat, shrimp, and scallops in a bowl and very gently mix together. Add the mayonnaise mixture and fold all together.

Spread the fillets with the seafood mixture and roll up. Arrange seam side down in a glass baking dish large enough to hold all the fillets.

Melt the remaining butter and brush the tops of the rolled fillets. Season lightly with salt and pepper. Top each fillet with a squeeze of juice from the remaining lemon. Pour the hot wine into the bottom of the baking dish. Cover the baking dish with aluminum foil and, with a sharp knife, make several slits to allow steam to escape.

Bake for 25 to 30 minutes, or until the fish is cooked through. Remove the fillets with a slotted spatula to a heated platter and keep warm while making the Lemon Butter sauce. When the sauce is ready, place the fillets on warmed dinner plates, lightly nap with Simple Lemon Butter, and serve immediately.

Simple Lemon Butter

4 tablespoons salted butter
Juice of 1 lemon
2 tablespoons chopped
    parsley

In a small sauté pan, melt the butter over medium heat. When the butter has melted completely, slightly increase the heat and add the lemon juice and parsley all at once. The butter will foam up slightly. Remove from heat and sauce the fillets at once.

When I was visiting my sister in Portland, Oregon, she brought home some fresh halibut and some very early spring peas. This is the dish that resulted, and I think that when fresh peas and delicately flavored halibut meet, it is nothing short of a Pacific Northwest culinary Nirvana.

Halibut with Herbed Fennel Butter and Sweet Peas

This recipe may appear a bit daunting, but it is not really difficult. The trick is to prepare it in stages:

1. Partially cook the peas.

2. Make a fairly basic shallot butter sauce, with lots of ingredients.

3. Cook the fish fillets in a pan.

4. Put 1, 2, and 3 together on a plate.

I assure you it is well worth the effort for a meal that will wow your guests, and make you feel the consummate chef.

Serves 4

FOR THE PEAS:

1 cup fresh peas (frozen sweet peas will also work)
1 tablespoon unsalted butter, softened
1 teaspoon finely chopped fennel leaves
1 teaspoon fresh lemon juice
Pinch of salt

FOR THE HERBED FENNEL BUTTER SAUCE:

8 tablespoons (1 stick) unsalted butter, cut into small pieces
1 tablespoon minced garlic
1 tablespoon minced shallots
$^1/_2$ cup minced fennel bulb
1 teaspoon finely chopped thyme
1 teaspoon finely chopped tarragon
1 large tomato, cored, seeded, and diced
$^3/_4$ cup Fish Stock (page 10)
$^1/_4$ cup dry white wine
6 tablespoons heavy whipping cream

PREPARE THE PEAS: In a pot of boiling, salted water, blanch the peas for about 2 minutes. Remove the peas immediately with a slotted spoon from boiling water and put them into ice water to stop the cooking process. Save the cooking water from the peas, as you will need it later to briefly reheat them. Drain the peas and set aside.

PREPARE THE SAUCE: In a small saucepan, melt 2 tablespoons of the butter and sauté the garlic, shallots, fennel, thyme, and tarragon. Cook over low heat for 3 to 4 minutes, stirring often so the vegetables do not brown. Remove the vegetables with a slotted spoon and set aside. Return saucepan to heat and add the tomato, fish stock, and white wine. Cook over medium heat until the volume reduces by half. Strain the mixture through a fine sieve into a bowl and clean out the saucepan. Add the strained liquid back to the saucepan along with the whipping cream. Reduce this mixture by half, about 5 minutes. With a wire whisk, add the remaining butter a few pieces at a time, stirring constantly. Continue until all the butter is incorporated and an emulsified sauce has formed. Add

FOR THE FISH:
4 tablespoons olive oil
Four 6-ounce halibut fillets
Kosher salt
Freshly ground black pepper

Fennel sprigs, for garnish
Lemon wedges, for garnish

the reserved vegetables and stir briefly to warm. Remove sauce from heat and set aside in a warm spot until the fish is cooked.

COOK THE FISH: Heat olive oil in a sauté pan large enough to hold the fillets. Season the halibut with salt and pepper to taste on both sides. When the oil is very hot, carefully place the fillets, skin side up, into the sauté pan and cook over medium-high heat for about 3 minutes. Carefully turn over the fillets in the pan and continue cooking another 3 minutes, or until just cooked. The inside of the fish should not be translucent and should flake easily. Do not overcook.

FINAL ASSEMBLY: While the fish is cooking, reheat the water in which the peas were cooked. While the water is heating, mix the butter and fennel leaves together with the lemon juice and salt. Drop the peas into the hot water and reheat for 1 minute. Strain and toss the peas with the butter mixture to coat. Set aside.

When the fish is finished cooking, place each fillet on a heated dinner plate. Spoon the herb butter over and around the fillets. Arrange the peas around the fish so that some spill into the sauce. Garnish with fennel sprigs and lemon wedges.

Try saying the name of this recipe three times quickly! Grouper is an extremely popular catch from the Gulf of Mexico for the folks living in Corpus Christi, Texas. The lean, firm-fleshed fillets are best prepared simply. Corpus Christi native Christopher Aeby, chef/owner of his innovative local restaurant Lavender, whips up a colorful Cilantro-Lime Vinaigrette for the fish. The vinaigrette is delightful on its own and could easily become a staple in my collection of "favorite" vinaigrettes.

Chris suggests serving Bacon Roasted Potatoes (page 219) and Chris's Cumin Carrots (page 207) with the grouper.

Corpus Christi Crispy Grouper with Cilantro-Lime Vinaigrette

Serves 4

Four 6-ounce grouper fillets
Salt
1/4 cup vegetable oil
Cilantro-Lime Vinaigrette
(recipe below)

Pat the fish dry and sprinkle the skin side with salt to taste. Heat the oil in a sauté pan on medium-high heat. Cook the fish skin side down until the edges of the fish start to brown. Turn the fish over and turn off the heat. Allow to rest for 4 minutes in the pan. Total cooking time should be 7 to 10 minutes; fish should be just opaque all the way through. To serve, drizzle with vinaigrette.

Cilantro-Lime Vinaigrette

1/4 cup white wine vinegar
1 small shallot, minced
1 scant teaspoon Dijon
    mustard
Pinch of powdered coriander
1 lime, zested, seeded, and
    juiced
1/4 cup chopped cilantro
Salt
1 1/4 cups grapeseed oil

Mix together the vinegar, shallot, mustard, coriander, lime zest and juice, cilantro, and salt to taste. Whisk in the oil slowly, a little at a time. Adjust seasoning if necessary.

When I listened to it as a child, Glen Campbell's song "Galveston" always conjured images for me of a sleepy Gulf town lined with oil rigs. On my first visit, I was delighted to find no oil rigs in the city, but rather a charming, Victorian-style town. Making my way down the main thoroughfare, Broadway, I headed for the historic East End. There I stumbled upon a wonderful urban American café that dishes up fresh, clean, original Gulf fare. The Mosquito Café serves an amazing variety of salads and sandwiches, but also regularly features seafood specials.

This grouper dish is simple to prepare and is topped with Nectarine and Red Onion Relish. It is uncooked and makes a refreshing topping for just about any grilled fish, or even a chicken breast.

Mosquito Café Grilled Grouper with Nectarine and Red Onion Relish

Serves 6

Six 8-ounce grouper fillets
(see note)
1/2 cup olive oil
Salt and freshly ground black
pepper
Nectarine and Red Onion
Relish (recipe follows)

Prepare a charcoal grill. Pat the fillets dry, brush generously with the olive oil, and season to taste with salt and pepper. Place the fish on an oiled rack set about 6 inches over glowing coals for 4 to 5 minutes on each side, or until opaque in the center. Transfer to plates and top with relish. Serve with Gulf Coast Peach-Pecan Couscous (page 220) and fresh asparagus.

NOTE: You may use any other "meaty" white fish, such as mahi mahi or orange roughy.

Nectarine and Red Onion Relish

1 red bell pepper, seeded and
cut into thin strips
6 ripe but firm nectarines,
cut into thin slices
1 medium red onion, sliced
into thin strips
$1/2$ teaspoon minced garlic
3 tablespoons chopped fresh
basil
$1/4$ cup red wine vinegar
$1/4$ cup orange juice
$1/2$ cup extra virgin olive oil
1 tablespoon kosher salt
1 teaspoon freshly ground
white pepper

Place the bell pepper, nectarines, red onion, garlic, and basil in
a mixing bowl. In a small bowl, combine the red wine vinegar
and orange juice. Whisk in the olive oil and season with salt and
pepper. Pour the liquid over the nectarine mixture and gently
toss. Cover and let sit 30 minutes before using. The relish may
be refrigerated, but should be brought almost to room temperature before serving.

Lauderdale-by-the-Sea Grouper Reuben

I had always heard about the fun and sun—and wild times—of Fort Lauderdale. So to ease myself into the life, I thought it would be best to start with the more sedate community, slightly to the north, Lauderdale-by-the-Sea, a charming older, laid-back town with a 1960's aura. My friend Markie, a Lauderdale local, took me to his favorite seaside restaurant, Ocean's Edge, and we settled in at a table where you could dig your feet into the warm sand. I ordered the required conch chowder, and then tried a fish-style Reuben sandwich. Wow, was that good! I continued traveling throughout Florida, but needed to return to Ft. Lauderdale to fly home. Before I could get on the plane, we had to detour back to Ocean's Edge for one more Grouper Reuben to make the trip complete.

Serves 4

Four 6-ounce grouper or
   mahi mahi fillets
Vegetable oil, as needed
1/2 cup blackening seasoning
Softened butter, as needed
8 slices rye bread
1/2 cup Remoulade Sauce
   (page 131) or Russian
   dressing
8 slices Swiss cheese
1 cup Apple-Fennel Coleslaw
   (page 201), or other
   prepared coleslaw

Lightly brush the fish fillets with oil and then dust in the blackening seasoning. Grease the bottom of a large cast iron skillet with vegetable oil and heat until very hot, almost smoking hot. Place the fillets in the pan and cook until the underside appears charred, about 2 minutes. Turn the fillets over and cook until done, about 2 minutes longer. Cooking time may vary depending on the thickness of the fillets. Place the cooked fillets on a plate and set aside.

Butter one side of each slice of rye bread. Heat a flat-top grill or large skillet. Place 4 slices of bread on the hot surface, butter side down. Spoon the Remoulade Sauce on each slice. Place 1 slice of cheese on each piece and top with a fillet. Place about 2 tablespoons of coleslaw on top of the fish. Slather the remaining slices of bread with Remoulade Sauce on the unbuttered side. Place the remaining cheese on each sandwich and top with bread, leaving the buttered side up. Gently push down on each sandwich with a metal spatula. Cook for about 3 minutes on each side, or until both sides of the sandwich are nicely brown and the cheese begins to melt. Cut on an angle and serve at once.

Swedes in Fort Lauderdale? You betcha!

Catti Eriksson is a proud member of the Swedish Women's Education Association, which promotes preservation of Swedish culture to thousands of Swedes who made their way to the sunny Florida coast. They have adapted well to the laid-back Florida lifestyle and meet regularly—often traveling by boat—to prepare traditional Scandinavian dishes, this delicate-flavored gravlax being one of the favorites.

Catti's Lauderdale Gravlax with Dill Mustard Sauce

Serves a crowd as an appetizer

2 center-cut, skin-on salmon fillets (1 1/2 to 2 pounds total)
1/4 cup sugar
1/4 cup kosher salt
2 tablespoons coarsely crushed white peppercorns
2 bunches dill
Dill Mustard Sauce (recipe follows)
Dark bread, such as pumpernickel, for serving

Gravlax differs from smoked salmon in that it is cured instead of smoked, meaning it is rubbed with a salt/sugar mixture and allowed to "cure" (age) for several days or more. Coarsely ground black pepper may be used in place of the white, and I like to pat several tablespoons of cognac onto the fish after I have coated it with the seasoning mixture.

Remove all the fine bones from the salmon fillets with tweezers.

Mix the sugar, salt, and peppercorns together. Rub the fillets with the mixture. Place the dill on top of the fillets.

Pair the fillets meat sides together. Wrap salmon in a plastic bag and place on a tray or in a shallow glass baking dish. Place a flat pan or dish on top of the fish and put a weighted object, such as a 5-pound bag of sugar or a large can, on top.

Let the fish "cure" in the refrigerator for about 2 to 3 days with the weight on it. Turn the fish twice daily. Remove the gravlax from the dish and pat it dry. Remove the whole pieces of dill and with a very sharp knife slice the fillets thinly on the diagonal, detaching each slice from the skin. Serve with Dill Mustard Sauce and dark bread.

Dill Mustard Sauce

$1/2$ cup honey mustard

1 to 2 teaspoons Dijon
mustard

1 tablespoon sugar

1 tablespoon white wine
vinegar

$1^1/2$ cups vegetable oil

$1/2$ cup finely chopped fresh
dill

Salt and freshly ground white
pepper

Mix the mustards, sugar, and vinegar in a nonreactive bowl. Add the oil, whisking to form an emulsion. Season with dill and salt and pepper to taste.

Roasting wild salmon is a tradition dating back many hundreds of years in the Pacific Northwest. During a visit to Seattle, my friend Mary McGowan and I took a boat ride to Blake Island in Elliott Bay to experience an authentic re-creation of a Native American salmon roast.

Wildwood Planked Salmon

It is an arduous process in which round pits are dug for fires and stoked with hardwood. Sides of salmon are affixed to split wood planks and placed near the open fire to roast slowly. It is great fun to watch and a memorable experience to sit at long family-style tables enjoying platters of freshly roasted salmon.

Serves 4

4 cedar planks, soaked overnight in water (see note)
Four 6-ounce salmon fillets, preferably wild, boned, skins on
Vegetable oil
Salt and freshly ground black pepper
8 sprigs fresh rosemary, thyme, or tarragon

No one is going to want to replicate this at home, and there is no need to with this planked salmon recipe by one of the Pacific Northwest's best known and most highly acclaimed chefs, Cory Schreiber of Portland, Oregon. At his hip regional restaurant, Wildwood, where the finest of Pacific Northwest fare is celebrated, Cory uses a technique that is much more manageable for the home cook, but still imparts the wonderful wood scent to the baked salmon fillets. Cory, author of Wildwood: Cooking from the Source in the Pacific Northwest, *suggests serving the salmon with Saffron-Braised Leeks (page 208).*

Preheat the oven to 400°F.

Drain the cedar planks. Lightly coat the salmon with vegetable oil and season with salt and pepper to taste. Place the salmon on the planks, tucking 2 herb sprigs underneath each fillet. Bake for 15 to 20 minutes, or until the salmon is firm to the touch. For an attractive presentation, serve the salmon on the boards, which may darken in the oven.

NOTE: You can find cedar grilling planks at gourmet speciality stores. You can also find cedar scraps at lumberyards and home-improvement centers, but you must be certain to use only new natural cedar, and not other wood scraps, possibly treated with preservative chemicals.

SALMON—WILD, FARMED, AND THE ROAST   Among finfish, the salmon is our national icon. Found in lakes, rivers, and oceans, the fish make migratory runs each year from their saltwater habitat upstream to fresh water to spawn. From the Pacific Northwest waters come varieties such as king, coho, silver, and sockeye. And on the east coast, the Atlantic salmon, with its pink, succulent flesh, is not only fished in the wild, but farmed as well. (Most salmon connoisseurs will agree that wild salmon possess a far more complex and satisfactory flavor than their farm-raised cousins.)

The salmon is legendary in historic recipes and accounts that predate the arrival of New World colonists. Native Americans revered the salmon and it figured prominently in lore and spiritual traditions.

While I was visiting Seattle, Washington, I had the opportunity to take a sail across the Sound to Tillicum Village, located on Blake Island, where the Northwest Native American tradition is still celebrated. Every year, thousands of people visit the "longhouse," which is styled after the ancient dwellings of native tribes. Large sides of salmon are butterflied, sandwiched between cross-sticks, and attached to cedar stakes. The stakes are stuck into the ground in a circle, slightly angled toward a huge alder-wood blaze in the center. It's a spectacular experience to see and smell the slowly roasting wild Pacific salmon. Guests are then treated to ample helpings of the freshly roasted smoked salmon, red "new" potatoes, and the village's delectable, molasses-scented, whole-grain bread. It's a four-hour voyage to another era and a peek into an almost vanished way of life.

This gingered marinade for salmon is a staple in San Diego. Edie Greenberg, food writer, cooking instructor, and food guru to southern California, says "everybody" in San Diego uses this marinade "on everything." I prefer using wild salmon. It costs a bit more, but tastes better and is even better for you than farm-raised salmon. Better for the environment, too.

Edie's Gingered Salmon

Serves 4

Four 6-ounce salmon fillets
Gingered Marinade (recipe follows)

Preheat the broiler.

Place the salmon fillets in a broiler pan. Spoon marinade over fish and broil until nicely browned, 4 to 5 minutes per inch of thickness of fish for medium rare. If the top of the fish seems to be cooking too quickly, place it in the oven at 350°F to finish. Do not overcook.

Gingered Marinade

One 1½-inch piece of fresh
  ginger, peeled
2 tablespoons canola oil
3 tablespoons finely chopped
  green onion, green and
  white parts
¼ cup soy sauce (not low
  sodium)
1 tablespoon sugar
1 teaspoon mirin (Japanese
  sweet cooking wine)
1 teaspoon sesame oil

I've tried this marinade with tuna, swordfish, shark, and moonfish (opah) fillets, and it is fantastic. Depending on the intensity of the ginger flavor you want, adjust the amount of time the marinade interacts with the fish: For example, for a very light taste, simply brush it on; or for a stronger flavor, pour a little of the marinade in a glass or ceramic dish and marinate the fillets for about ten minutes on each side. I would not allow the fish to rest in the marinade any longer than thirty minutes.

Process the ginger in a food processor until finely chopped.

Heat the canola oil in a skillet and add the ginger and green onion. Cook until lightly browned, stirring with a wooden spoon. Remove from heat and cool. The mixture tends to stick to the pan but will come loose when cool.

In a separate bowl, combine the soy sauce, sugar, mirin, and sesame oil and mix well. Blend in onion-ginger mixture. If not using immediately, transfer the mixture to a jar and refrigerate until needed.

This is a beautiful dish, which is quite fitting, given that it is from the breathtakingly beautiful San Ysidro Ranch, nestled in the lush foothills overlooking Santa Barbara, California. A more romantic spot would be hard to find. It's so romantic that this is where John and Jackie Kennedy spent their honeymoon, not to mention where Sir Laurence Olivier and Vivien Leigh exchanged their wedding vows. The resort boasts an amazing kitchen as well, and the creative force behind it is executive chef Jamie West. Jamie alters his menus frequently to reflect the change of seasons and the bounty of the ranch's own organic gardens.

San Ysidro Ranch Wild Salmon with Potato–Fava Bean Salad

Serves 4

5 tablespoons olive oil
1 pound small red potatoes, cooked until just tender, cooled and sliced
2 tablespoons thinly sliced shallots
4 slices applewood-smoked bacon, chopped, cooked until crisp
1 roma tomato, finely diced
$1/2$ small fennel bulb, trimmed, thinly sliced, fronds reserved for garnish
$1/2$ cup fava beans, removed from pod, briefly blanched, and cooled
Salt and freshly ground black pepper
Four 6-ounce salmon fillets
4 tablespoons chopped fresh tarragon
Tarragon Mustard Vinaigrette (recipe follows)
4 sprigs fresh tarragon, for garnish

Heat 3 tablespoons of the olive oil in a large skillet over medium heat. Add the potatoes and cook until they are slightly brown on the outside, stirring often. Add the shallots and bacon. Stir well. Cook another 3 minutes, until potatoes are soft, but not falling apart. Add the tomato, fennel, and blanched fava beans. Mix gently, being careful not to crush the beans. Remove from heat. Season to taste with salt and pepper. Set aside and keep warm.

Season the fish with the tarragon and salt and pepper to taste.

In a large skillet, heat the remaining 2 tablespoons of oil until hot and cook the salmon fillets for 3 to 4 minutes per side, or until salmon is golden to dark brown, slightly crispy, and barely opaque in the center.

To serve, divide the warm potato salad among four plates and place a piece of salmon on top of each one. Drizzle generously with Tarragon Mustard Vinaigrette. Garnish with tarragon sprigs and fresh fennel.

Tarragon Mustard Vinaigrette

2 tablespoons country-style
Dijon mustard
2 tablespoons Champagne
vinegar
2 tablespoons chopped fresh
tarragon leaves
1 teaspoon minced garlic
$^3/_4$ cup olive oil
Juice of $^1/_2$ lemon
Salt and freshly ground black
pepper

Place mustard, vinegar, tarragon, and garlic in a blender. With machine running, slowly add the oil to emulsify. With machine still running, add lemon juice and season to taste with salt and pepper.

Some of the best smoked salmon I have found was at Vinton and Charisse Waldron's Seabolt Smokehouse on Whidbey Island, about forty-five miles north of Seattle. A commercial fisherman, Vinton not only catches the fish but smokes it as well. Most of the year he fishes locally, but in July and August he packs up his gear and heads off to Bristol Bay in Alaska, which boasts the largest sockeye salmon run in the world, returning with a bounty of wild salmon. When you have immediate access to seafood that fresh, the smoked product is bound to be exceptional. I brought home a generous sample of great Seabolt Smokehouse Salmon and used it to fashion these delectable salmon cakes.

Seabolt Smokehouse Salmon Cakes

Serves 4

3 tablespoons butter
1/2 cup minced onions
1 garlic clove, minced
3 cups diced potatoes
1/2 teaspoon salt
1/3 pound smoked salmon,
   flaked into pieces
1 egg, beaten
1 tablespoon freshly squeezed
   lemon juice
Dash of Tabasco
3 tablespoons minced chives
Lemon wedges
4 tablespoons vegetable oil or
   bacon grease, for frying

Melt the butter in a small sauté pan. Add the onions and garlic and cook, stirring frequently, until golden brown, 5 to 6 minutes. Set aside.

Place the potatoes in a pan with the salt and cover with boiling water. Cook over medium heat until soft. Drain the potatoes well and place in a mixing bowl.

Add the smoked salmon to the potatoes and mash them together with a potato masher. Beat in the sautéed onions and egg. Add the lemon juice, Tabasco, and chives. Mix well and form into patties.

Heat oil or bacon grease in a heavy skillet or frying pan. Brown the cakes on both sides, about 2 1/2 minutes per side. Remove from the pan to paper towels to drain. Serve with lemon wedges.

A pharmacist by trade, My Phuong Huyng also happens to be the daughter of one of Vietnam's best chefs, the late Lan Huyng, the woman I called Mama Lan. My gets to use both her scientific and culinary skills in this dish—measuring, mixing, and reducing. This fantastic tuna preparation illustrates perfectly the melding of classic French cuisine with the cuisine of its former colony, Vietnam. The tuna is coated in a decorative fashion with the two types of sesame seed. The sauce is a French technique, a classic butter sauce, but this one starts with a reduction of aromatic Asian ingredients.

My Phuong's Black-and-White Sesame Tuna

Serves 4

Four 6-ounce tuna steaks, about 1 inch thick
Salt and freshly ground black pepper
1 cup white sesame seeds
1 cup black sesame seeds
2 teaspoons vegetable oil
Orange-Soy Sauce (recipe follows)

Sprinkle the tuna steaks with salt and pepper. Carefully pour half of the white sesame seeds on one side of a plate, and half of the black seeds on the other side. The two colors of seeds should meet in the center, but not overlap. (Use a piece of paper or a strip of foil to keep the seeds separate while pouring, then gently push them together to meet.) Place each steak in the center of the plate and press down to make the seeds stick. Turn over and repeat. Renew seeds as necessary.

Put the oil in a cast iron skillet over high heat. When the pan is very hot, add the tuna steaks, cooking them for $1^1/2$ to 2 minutes per side, depending on how rare you like them (with $1^1/2$ minutes being very rare). Serve hot, topped with Orange-Soy Sauce.

Orange-Soy Sauce

2 tablespoons Chinese black
   soy sauce (see note)
1 teaspoon grated ginger
$1/8$ teaspoon freshly ground
   black pepper
Zest of 1 orange
$1/4$ cup orange juice
$1/4$ cup Fish Stock (page 10)
8 tablespoons (1 stick) butter,
   cut in small pieces

Place the soy sauce, ginger, pepper, orange zest, orange juice, and fish stock in a saucepan over medium heat and cook until reduced by half, about 5 minutes. Reduce heat to low and whisk in the butter, one small piece at a time, until it is all incorporated.

NOTE: Chinese soy sauce is made "black" with the addition of molasses. It can be found at Asian markets and gourmet specialty shops.

Jay Moore, chef/owner of AransaZu restaurant, is living his dream and establishing his vision in the small Texas coastal town of Rockport. This is thankfully a not-too-gentrified artist community about thirty miles northeast of Corpus Christi, a place Jay fondly dubs the "Redneck Riviera." It's a slow-paced town nestled behind the barrier islands on the Gulf of Mexico with vibrant galleries, commercial and recreational fishing, and a pristine National Wildlife Refuge—"a wonderful place to raise the kids." Jay wasn't always this laid back; in fact, he was in high gear up in Austin, Texas, as the co-owner and chef of the renowned Hudson's on the Bend restaurant, where he coauthored Cooking Fearlessly: Recipes and Other Adventures from Hudson's on the Bend.

Jay may have slowed down a bit, but he's still in Texas. Even on the Gulf Coast, folks think of their fish in terms of beef—thus the "prime rib." What we actually have here is a tuna loin that is wrapped in smoked bacon and roasted in a very hot oven. The end result is smoky-flavored, meaty slices of rare tuna accompanied by a Wasabi Cream Sauce that is so good that even if you did not have any tuna, you would find yourself dipping in tortilla chips and raw veggies. Jay actually prepares this recipe party-style—meaning he uses a six- or seven-pound loin, has a bunch of people over, and slices it like prime rib. Should you decide to increase the poundage, also increase the roasting time to six minutes per pound.

Roast "Prime Rib" of Tuna with Wasabi Cream Sauce

Serves 6 to 8

½ pound bacon
3 pounds trimmed tuna loin
Kosher salt
Wasabi Cream Sauce (recipe follows)

Preheat the oven to 475°F.

Place bacon slices between two pieces of plastic wrap and pound with a mallet or a sauté pan until thin. Refrigerate until ready to use.

Pat the tuna loin dry and season lightly with salt. Remove top layer of plastic wrap from the bacon. Lay the tuna loin in the center of the bacon and use the plastic to help guide the bacon around the tuna. Remove the plastic and discard.

Place bacon-wrapped tuna in a lightly oiled roasting pan and roast approximately 5 minutes per pound. Remove from the oven, and loosely cover the loin with foil. Allow tuna to rest 10 minutes before slicing.

Serve with Asian-style rice and Wasabi Cream Sauce.

Wasabi Cream Sauce

2 tablespoons wasabi paste
   (see note)
One 1^1/2-inch piece peeled
   fresh ginger, minced
1 garlic clove, minced
4 green onions, thinly sliced
1 tablespoon rice wine
   vinegar
1 teaspoon soy sauce
6 to 8 drops of sesame oil
1 cup heavy cream, chilled

Combine all ingredients and beat to stiff peaks.

NOTE: Wasabi paste is available in Japanese markets and gourmet shops. Wasabi is known as Japanese horseradish and has a fiery, pungent quality.

ROCKPORT-FULTON, TEXAS

The cities of Rockport and Fulton, Texas, combined population of about 8,500, sit quietly on the delightful and unexpected Texas Gulf Coast. These two towns are hospitable to fishing, boating, artists, and wildlife, and are noted for their beaches and the Texas Maritime Museum. The area is right on the migratory Central Flyway, and is noted for its songbirds, shorebirds, waterfowl, and birds of prey— so far, 500 different species have been counted.

Floridians love to grill. And it doesn't take much to turn out a fantastic meal: fresh fish, a brushing with oil or brightly flavored marinade, and onto the grill. Michelle Bernstein, a native of Miami and one of the city's top chefs, enjoys grilling snapper for family and friends. She serves it with a sofrito, which is spicy, pungent, and an ideal accent to the grilled snapper.

The sofrito recipe calls for aji Amarillo, a long, cylindrical chile with pods that have a crisp, citrus aroma. It can be found in Hispanic markets and specialty shops. Serve with Cuban-Style Black Beans (page 211), rice, and perhaps some fried plantains.

Whole Roasted Red Snapper with Sofrito

Serves 4

1 whole snapper, 2 to 3
   pounds
Olive oil
Salt and freshly ground black
   pepper
Sofrito (recipe follows)

Heat the grill. Preheat the oven to 350°F.

Cut out the center bones of the snapper, keeping the head and tail intact. Brush with olive oil, season with salt and pepper to taste, and place on hot grill. Cook for 3 to 4 minutes on each side.

Place the fish in an ovenproof dish and bake for 5 to 8 minutes to finish cooking. The fish should be cooked through, opaque, and flaky. Top with Sofrito and serve.

Sofrito

2 tablespoons olive oil
1 yellow bell pepper, minced
1 red bell pepper, minced
1 red onion, minced
1 large tomato, diced
4 garlic cloves, minced
$^{1}/_{2}$ Scotch bonnet pepper,
    minced (see note)
1 tablespoon minced aji
    Amarillo
1 small fennel bulb, minced
Pinch of saffron
1 cup dry white wine
1 cup Fish Stock (page 10) or
    clam juice
1 bunch cilantro (pick leaves
    and chop stems)
1 lime

In a saucepan, heat the olive oil on medium-high heat. Add all the vegetables. Cook, stirring frequently, for 5 to 6 minutes, or until the vegetables are slightly soft.

Add the saffron and the wine and reduce by half, about 5 minutes. Add the stock and again reduce by half, about another 5 minutes. Finish with cilantro and a squeeze of lime.

Place half the sofrito in a blender and puree. Combine the pureed sofrito with the chunky sofrito and immediately serve over the fish.

NOTE: Wear gloves when handling chiles and do not touch bare skin. In place of aji Amarillo, increase the Scotch bonnet pepper to 1 whole pepper and add the zest of $^{1}/_{2}$ lemon.

LATIN MIAMI

Half the population of Miami is Latin, so it's not surprising that the city is home to two vibrant neighborhoods that embody the culture of the countries where many of the inhabitants were born: Little Havana and Little Haiti.

Little Havana is spread out along Southwest 8th Street, called in the district simply Calle Ocho. The street is lined with shops and restaurants, all catering to the Cuban population. You can smell the aroma of the sweetly intense café Cubano—Cuban coffee, made with dark-roast beans and lots of sugar—as it wafts over the street, and you can hear the sizzle of Cuban-style fried chicken being prepared. Cuban food, which is based on a Spanish culinary heritage, is flavorful and robust but not generally highly spiced.

The heart of Little Haiti is at Northeast 54th Street, a few blocks west of Biscayne Boulevard. The neighborhood is home to the largest

Haitian population in the United States, and retains the customs and flavors of the island to the south in its shops, restaurants, and boutiques. Little Haiti is also home to the Caribbean Marketplace, an award-winning replica of the open-air Iron Market in Port-au-Prince. Haitian cooking is based more on island and African influences, and uses lots of piquant ingredients, such as chiles, garlic, and star anise. Haitians are proud of their fish (see Miss Liliane's Haitian-Style Flounder, page 88) and their *lambi,* or conch (see Puffy Conch Fritters, page 164).

I had heard that there was a thriving Haitian community in the Miami area and set my sights on one of its most prominent personalities, Liliane Nerette Louis. Miss Liliane is co-author of the book When Night Falls, Kric! Krac!: Haitian Folktales—*a delightful compilation of Haitian folktales, lore, and cuisine, full of warmth and wit. She is a remarkable woman who has been at the forefront in preserving the culture of Haiti. In addition to her book, she produced a special focusing on the Haitian community for Florida public television.*

When I found Liliane, she graciously welcomed me into her home, and in a matter of minutes we were in the kitchen where she works culinary magic. Miss Liliane is passionate about her cooking and the traditional techniques used in her homeland.

Fish obviously plays a large role in the culture and cuisine of the island of Haiti, and in this recipe I've used some of the techniques and ingredients that Liliane teaches her students.

Miss Liliane's Haitian-Style Flounder

Serves 6

Six 6-ounce flounder fillets
2 limes
3 tablespoons chopped flat-leaf parsley, plus more for garnish
Salt
4 tablespoons ($^1/_2$ stick) butter
4 tablespoons olive oil
1 small onion, finely chopped
1 tablespoon minced garlic
1 small red bell pepper, finely chopped
1 small serrano chile pepper, finely chopped
3 tomatoes, peeled, seeded, and chopped
$^1/_3$ cup freshly squeezed orange juice
Freshly ground black pepper
Lime wedges
Steamed white or jasmine rice for serving

Rinse the fillets with cold water mixed with the juice of 1 lime. Pat dry and place the flounder on a plate. Squeeze the juice of the second lime over the fillets and sprinkle with chopped parsley and lightly salt. Set aside.

In a sauté pan large enough to hold all the fillets, melt the butter and add the olive oil. Sauté the onion, garlic, red bell pepper, and chile over medium heat until vegetables begin to soften, about 3 minutes. Add the tomatoes and orange juice and season with salt and pepper to taste. Bring the sauce to a boil, and add the fish fillets and about $^1/_2$ cup water. Lower the heat to medium and continue simmering (basting frequently) gently for about 10 minutes, or until the fish begins to flake. Carefully remove the fillets with a slotted spatula and place each fillet on a warmed dinner plate. Spoon the sauce from the pan over each serving and garnish fish with chopped parsley and lime wedges. Serve with steamed white or jasmine rice.

Brasa means "live coals" in Portuguese, and that is just how chef Tamara Murphy cooks at Brasa, her Seattle restaurant—with live coals. It makes for fantastic-tasting local seafood and meats. When she's not manning her spatula, Tamara likes to rough it, kayaking and fly-fishing in the wilds of the Pacific Northwest.

Moroccan Pesto Sturgeon with Clam and Chorizo Sauce

Tamara says to be authentic, you should prepare the pesto in the Moroccan way, by pounding the ingredients in a mortar with a pestle. Most people don't have the patience for that, and besides, it's hard work. This is why food processors were invented. If sturgeon isn't available, substitute striped bass or rockfish.

Serves 4

1/3 cup chopped parsley
1/3 cup chopped cilantro
2 garlic cloves
1 tablespoon toasted cumin
  seed (see note)
2 tablespoons freshly
  squeezed lemon juice
Salt
4 tablespoons extra virgin
  olive oil
Four 6-ounce sturgeon fillets
Clam and Chorizo Sauce
  (recipe follows)
1 green onion, slivered, for
  garnish

MORTAR AND PESTLE METHOD:

Place the parsley, cilantro, garlic, cumin, lemon juice, and salt to taste in a large mortar with a little of the olive oil and pound into a paste with a pestle. Add the remaining olive oil. Slather mixture on the fish and refrigerate for up to 2 hours.

FOOD PROCESSOR METHOD:

Place the parsley, cilantro, garlic, cumin, lemon juice, salt to taste, and 1 tablespoon of the olive oil in the bowl of a food processor. Pulse until the mixture forms a paste. Add the remaining olive oil, a tablespoon or so at a time, and pulse to mix well. Slather on the fish and refrigerate for up to 2 hours.

Heat the grill.

Remove the sturgeon fillets from the refrigerator and cook them on the grill for approximately 4 to 5 minutes per side, depending on the thickness of the fillet. Fish should be cooked through until opaque and flaky for best flavor.

To serve, place the cooked fillets on a platter, and place the clams around them. Spoon the sauce over the fish and garnish with green onion slivers.

NOTE: To toast cumin seeds, preheat the oven to 400°F. Spread the seeds on a baking sheet and cook until fragrant, 3 to 4 minutes.

Clam and Chorizo Sauce

3 tablespoons extra virgin
    olive oil
1 tablespoon minced shallots
1 tablespoon minced garlic
1 pound chorizo, or other
    flavorful sausage,
    crumbled
$1/2$ cup chopped tomatoes
12 to 20 small clams (3 to 5
    per person)
$1/2$ cup white wine
Salt and freshly ground black
    pepper
Juice of 1 lemon

Heat the olive oil in a large pot or sauté pan. Add the shallots and garlic and cook on low heat for 1 minute. Add the sausage and cook through. Add the tomatoes, clams, and wine, and cook until the clams open. (Discard any that don't open.) Season to taste with salt, pepper, and lemon juice.

In the Mid-Atlantic we refer to striped bass as rockfish, and it is some fine eating. About fifteen years ago, the rockfish population went into a horrific decline, and it appeared that it might be the end for the region's most popular finfish. However, a moratorium on both commercial and recreational fishing was put on the species. A number of years later, the rockfish rebounded and now thrives in record numbers. This recipe is rooted in the Eastern Shore tradition of the Chesapeake and has a moist, dense, puddinglike seafood stuffing. There is no fancy sauce needed here—just the fish from the pan and a squeeze of lemon.

Rockfish with Shrimp and Crab Cornbread Stuffing

Serves 4 to 5

4 tablespoons ($^1/_2$ stick) butter
$^1/_2$ cup diced onion
$^1/_2$ cup diced fennel bulb
$^1/_2$ cup diced carrot
$^1/_2$ teaspoon minced garlic
1 pound lump crabmeat, picked over for shells
$^1/_2$ pound steamed shrimp, cut into bite-size pieces
2 cups crumbled South of the Mason-Dixon Line Cornbread (page 230)
2 eggs, lightly beaten
Salt and freshly ground black pepper
$^1/_4$ cup milk, plus more as needed
Vegetable oil
1 whole rockfish ($3^1/_2$ to 4 pounds), head off, boned
4 to 5 strips bacon
Lemon wedges

Melt the butter in a skillet and sauté the onion for about 2 minutes. Add the fennel, carrot, and garlic and continue to cook for 5 minutes longer, stirring often.

In a large mixing bowl, gently mix together the crabmeat and cooked shrimp. Add the crumbled cornbread, sautéed vegetables, and eggs. Toss gently, taking care not to break up the lumps of crab. Season the stuffing with salt and pepper to taste. Sprinkle the $^1/_4$ cup milk over the stuffing and retoss.

Preheat the oven to 375°F.

Lightly oil the bottom of a baking dish large enough to hold the fish.

Mound the stuffing inside the fish and smooth the outside to insure the stuffing stays in the fish during baking. Sprinkle the top of the fish with salt and pepper to taste. Wrap the bacon around the fish. Pour enough milk into pan to bring it to a depth of about $^1/_4$ inch.

Cover the baking dish with foil and bake for 30 minutes. Remove from the oven and take off the foil. Return to the oven and bake for 15 minutes longer, or until the fish flakes at the touch of a fork.

When done, transfer the fish to a serving platter. Pour any remaining cooking liquid over the fish and serve with lemon wedges.

Waterfront Market's Key Lime Mustard Sauce was originally developed as a dipping sauce for the local stone crab claws. They soon discovered their Key West customers were using it in a wide variety of ways. Most popular has been with fish, be it grouper, snapper, dolphin, or wahoo caught locally, or salmon, catfish, cod, and mackerel from afar. The sauce is amazingly versatile, perfect for grilling, baking, and broiling. It's great on shrimp and spiny lobster, fried seafood, and smoked fish, too. Or, try it as a binder for crab cakes and potato salad, or dolloped on baked potatoes or asparagus. Lauren, the seafood manager at Waterfront Market, says "for a little zip," add some drained horseradish to taste. And yes, it is great as a dip for stone crab claws.

Grilled Swordfish with Key Lime Mustard Sauce

Serves 4

1 cup mayonnaise
$1/4$ cup whole-grain mustard
1 tablespoon Key lime juice, fresh or bottled
$1/8$ teaspoon green hot sauce
4 swordfish steaks, about $1/2$-inch thick
Salt and freshly ground black pepper

Combine the mayonnaise, mustard, Key lime juice, and hot sauce in a bowl and mix well. Cover and set aside until ready to use. (The sauce will keep for weeks in the fridge.)

Season the swordfish with salt and pepper and place in a glass baking dish. Pour about $1/2$ cup of the Key Lime Mustard Sauce over the top and turn several times to coat well. Cover and place in the refrigerator for 30 to 40 minutes, turning once during the marinating process.

Heat the grill while the fish is marinating. Grill swordfish on hot grill for $1^{1}/2$ to 2 minutes per side, depending on the thickness of the steak. Serve at once with the remaining mustard sauce on the side.

When I had my restaurant, Gertie's, in Berkeley, California, my fishmonger, Kevin McCurdy, called one day to see if I was interested in buying some "beautiful Hawaiian moonfish." I'd never heard of this fish before, but I was so enchanted by the name I bought ten pounds on the spot. It was as good as it sounds. This fish, also called opah, is a full-flavored, pinkish fish found in warm waters, like those around Hawaii. Like tuna, moonfish can get to be huge—up to 200 pounds.

Steamed Moonfish with Sesame-Chile Sauce and Garlic Spinach

Serves 4

Sesame-Chile Sauce (recipe follows)
Four 6-ounce moonfish fillets, or other firm-fleshed fish, such as snapper
2 tablespoons olive oil
2 tablespoons minced garlic
8 cups fresh spinach leaves, stemmed, rinsed
Salt and freshly ground black pepper
3 tablespoons chopped green onion, for garnish
4 sprigs fresh cilantro leaves, for garnish

Make the Sesame-Chile Sauce and set aside.

Place the moonfish fillets in a steamer basket over simmering water. Cover and steam for about 5 minutes, or until fish is opaque in center and flakes easily.

While the fish is steaming, heat the olive oil in a saucepan. Add the garlic and cook for 10 seconds, toss in the spinach, cover, and cook for 2 minutes, stirring once, until spinach is just wilted, but not mushy. Season with salt and pepper.

To serve, divide spinach evenly in center of four plates. Place moonfish fillets on top, and drizzle with the Sesame-Chile Sauce. Sprinkle with chopped green onion and garnish with cilantro.

Sesame-Chile Sauce

1/3 cup sesame oil
2 teaspoons minced fresh ginger
1 Thai chile (see note)
1 tablespoon chopped green onion
1/4 cup soy sauce

Heat the sesame oil in a small skillet or saucepan and sauté the ginger, chile, and green onion briefly, about 10 seconds. Off heat, slowly add the soy sauce. (It may sizzle up, so take care not to be burned.) Return to heat and bring to a boil. Remove from heat and set aside. If necessary, reheat before using.

NOTE: Wear gloves when handling chiles and do not touch bare skin.

Catfish has some culinary detractors (you know—food snobs), but for my money it is some of the best southern coastal cooking to be found. Catfish is everywhere these days, as most of it is farm-raised, but I grew up on the wild variety found in the slow-moving, brackish rivers in the South. To some, the flavor of the farmed is preferable because it has a cleaner taste. To each their own, as my Aunt Minnie would always remind me, but I like the earthy (not muddy) quality of the wild catfish.

Pan-Fried Pan-Pan-Fried Catfish with Shrimp Creole Sauce

Serves 6

Leroy's Punta Gorda Shrimp Creole (page 158) (see note)
Six 6-ounce catfish fillets
Milk, as needed
1 cup all-purpose flour
1 cup finely ground yellow or white cornmeal
1 tablespoon Cajun seasoning
$1/2$ teaspoon cayenne pepper
Salt and freshly ground black pepper
Vegetable oil, for frying
Chopped flat-leaf parsley, for garnish
Lemon wedges, for garnish

The rendition we have here places the crisp fillets on a bed of spicy shrimp Creole—an unbelievably delicious marriage. However, this is a fine master recipe for basic fried catfish and you may prefer to serve it with Tasty Tartar Sauce (page 107) or a classic Remoulade Sauce (page 131). Or, for a real down-home experience, serve it with Dottie's Old Time Mac and Cheese (page 221).

Prepare the Shrimp Creole.

Soak the catfish fillets in milk to cover in a shallow dish for 1 hour.

In a second dish, mix the flour, cornmeal, Old Bay or Cajun seasoning, cayenne, and salt and pepper to taste. Remove the fish from the milk, 1 fillet at a time, letting the excess milk drip back into the dish. Coat well with the cornmeal mixture.

Pour oil into a skillet to a depth of $1/2$-inch and place over medium heat. When the oil is hot, add as many fillets as the pan will allow. Fry about 3 to 4 minutes on each side, or until golden brown. Remove fish from the pan and drain well on paper towels.

On a warmed dinner plate, make a bed of hot Shrimp Creole and place a fillet on top. Garnish with chopped flat-leaf parsley and lemon wedges. Simple white rice and greens are a perfect accompaniment, and don't forget to have freshly baked South of the Mason-Dixon Line Cornbread (page 230) on hand.

NOTE: When preparing the Shrimp Creole for use in this recipe, I often substitute small shrimp in place of the larger ones called for in the recipe. I find it works better for this dish. Another option would be to cut the larger shrimp into several pieces before cooking.

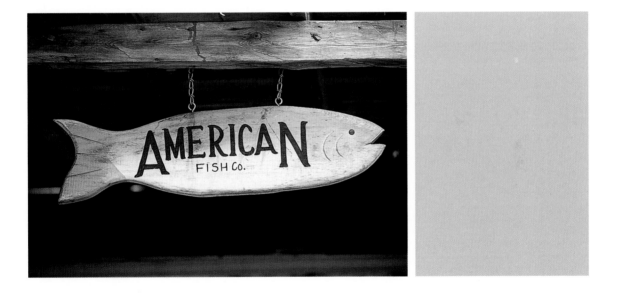

Rhode Island is known for superb seafood, usually served with an ethnic flair. There are sizeable Italian and Portuguese communities, and the influence of the homeland cuisines is still quite evident. Both groups cook up lots of squid, sometimes referred to by its Italian name, calamari. Squid can be stuffed with breading and braised in white wine or fresh tomato sauce, simmered into delicious stews, or—and this is the most popular—fried. Clean, crisp squid is normally served as an appetizer or snack with plenty of cold beer—definitely a tasty party food.

Prudence Island Fried Squid

Serves 4

1 pound cleaned squid
2 cups all-purpose flour
2 teaspoons salt
$1/2$ teaspoon freshly ground
    black pepper
$1/4$ teaspoon cayenne pepper
4 eggs, slightly beaten
3 cups fresh breadcrumbs
Vegetable oil for frying
Lemon wedges
Three Mustard Sauce (recipe
    follows)

Cut the cylindrical body of the squid into $1/4$-inch rings and the tentacles into small pieces.

In a bowl or baking dish, mix the flour, salt, pepper, and cayenne together. Place the eggs in another container and the breadcrumbs in a third container. Make an assembly line of flour mixture, eggs, and breadcrumbs.

Dust a few pieces of squid in the flour. Shake off excess and dip in the egg. Let a little of the egg drip off and then roll the squid in the breadcrumbs. Place breaded squid on a baking sheet lined with wax paper. Continue coating the remaining squid.

Pour vegetable oil into a skillet to a depth of about $1^1/2$ inches. Heat until quite hot, about 375°F. Fry the squid until golden brown, about 3 to 4 minutes. Do not overcrowd the pan and replace oil as needed after each batch. If oil is added, wait several minutes before frying the next batch, as the oil needs to come back to temperature.

Remove the squid from the pan to paper towels to drain. Serve immediately with lemon wedges and a bowl of Three Mustard Sauce for dipping.

Three Mustard Sauce

2 cups mayonnaise
$^1/_2$ cup Dijon mustard
$^1/_2$ cup coarse-grain mustard
1 tablespoon dry mustard
2 tablespoons horseradish
3 tablespoons Worcestershire
   sauce
$^1/_2$ teaspoon cayenne pepper
$^1/_2$ teaspoon freshly ground
   black pepper
1 teaspoon fresh lemon juice
$^1/_2$ teaspoon Tabasco

Place all the ingredients into a bowl and mix together well.

I had my first taste of this luscious, anchovy-scented casserole overlooking one of the numerous canals that flow throughout Fort Lauderdale. I'm not sure if it was the marvelous, comforting flavors and textures of Jansson's Temptation, or the wafting canal breezes and beautiful pastel villas that dot the banks, but this was one memorable dining experience. My hostess, Catti Eriksson, is a Swede who has spent more time aboard deck and galley kitchens than on dry land. She is well-known throughout Florida's Swedish community for this assertive, rich dish. The "temptation" is extremely popular in Sweden, but, according to Catti, actually originated here in the States. Add a simple salad of field greens, some warm dark bread, and a glass of beer—and life is good. A salt breeze doesn't hurt either.

Jansson's Temptation

Serves 6 to 8

1 can (2 ounces) anchovies in oil, drained, oil reserved
1 jar (4 ounces) matjes herring, drained, 3 tablespoons of liquid reserved (see note)
8 medium potatoes, peeled and sliced into $1/4$-inch slices
2 medium onions, peeled and thinly sliced
Salt and freshly ground black pepper
1 cup cream
$1/2$ cup milk
$1/2$ cup breadcrumbs
3 tablespoons butter, cut into small pieces

Preheat the oven to 425°F.

Dice the anchovies and matjes herring. Mix well with the oil from the anchovies and the reserved matjes liquid.

Grease a 9 x 13-inch ovenproof dish. Place a layer of potatoes on the bottom of the dish, followed by a layer of onions and a layer of anchovies and herring and a little salt and pepper. Keep alternating layers, finishing with a top layer of potatoes.

Mix together the cream and milk and pour half the mixture over the potatoes. Sprinkle half the breadcrumbs on top. Cover the dish with foil and place in the oven.

After 30 minutes, pour in the rest of the cream-milk mixture, sprinkle on the remaining breadcrumbs, and dot the top of the casserole with the butter. Place back into oven uncovered and bake for another 20 to 30 minutes, until the surface is nicely browned.

NOTE: Matjes are actually lightly salted "virgin" herring—meaning they have not yet spawned. They are quite popular throughout Scandinavia and northern Europe. If you can't locate matjes herring, use 4 more ounces of anchovies.

Each region boasts its own unique varieties of shellfish, some of the most popular denizens of the sea. New England has its lobster, scallops, and mussels, while the Mid-Atlantic is the land of the feisty blue crab, Chincoteague oysters, and soft-shell clams. Moving south, we encounter the stone crab of Florida, along with the conch, shrimp, and crayfish of the Gulf States. The Pacific coast has its own varieties of shrimp, such as the succulent Santa Barbara ridgeback, Monterey Bay prawns, and its own varieties of crab (the lumbering Dungeness crab and the gigantic Alaskan king crab), as

well as abalone, mussels, and an amazing variety of farm-raised oysters.

Shellfish is great when it's simple, as in boiled crabs

and steamed mussels, and equally wonderful when it's fancy, as in Maryland Eastern Shore crab cakes and mussels with smoked salmon and cream. It can be sauced with a simple bar-style tartar sauce, or a fancy New Orleans–style béarnaise. It can be eaten out of hand, like steamed shrimp, dug out of its shell if it's lobster or crab, and eaten as is or used as an ingredient in an elaborate dish.

Some shellfish dishes are legendary for their luxury, such as rich Smith Island Scalloped Oysters. And some are famous for their down-home qualities: think fried clams from New England. Shellfish is associated with good times and special occasions. It's absolutely not an accident that some kinds of shellfish preparations go by the name of "feast"—crab feasts, shrimp fests. And don't forget those southern crawdaddy and northern crab boils. Fact is, it's hard to have any kind of shellfish without turning dinner into a festival.

Joanne Turner-Slemp, a friend of mine since high school, found her old run-of-the-mill crab dip—you know, all mayonnaise and cheddar cheese—fine for the immediate family, but not exciting enough for her Chesapeake Bayside bashes. This curry-infused dip will enliven any party.

Jo-Jo's Curried Crab Dip

There are countless varieties of curry, and most curry lovers have their own combination of spices that they fashion into signature blends. Jo recommends Madras curry, which is readily available in most supermarkets and is spicy-hot. Any type of curry can be used in this recipe, and should you have an Indian food market nearby, experiment with different styles to get a good handle on the nuances of curry. One word of advice: Don't buy a large quantity, as curry loses its potency very quickly.

Serves about 8

1/2 cup dried currants
1 pound cream cheese, softened
2 tablespoons Madras curry powder
2 tablespoons mayonnaise
1/3 cup coconut milk
1/3 cup minced green onions or chives
1/3 cup finely diced red bell pepper
1 pound backfin or claw blue crabmeat
Crackers or gingersnaps, for serving

Preheat oven to 350°F.

Place the currants in a small bowl and add *just enough* boiling water to cover. Let stand for 15 minutes. Drain, reserving the liquid, and put the currants aside.

In a large bowl, combine the cream cheese, curry powder, mayonnaise, coconut milk, green onion, and red bell pepper. Beat until smooth and somewhat creamy. Mix in the crabmeat, currants, and reserved currant liquid.

Transfer the mixture to a greased casserole dish and bake for 25 to 30 minutes. Serve hot or warm with melba rounds, water crackers, or gingersnaps.

Shirley Phillips was raised on Hooper Island, Maryland, in Chesapeake Bay, and grew up surrounded by the finest seafood imaginable. Given her upbringing, it's not surprising that she married a waterman, Brice Phillips. The couple made their way to Ocean City, Maryland, and opened a crab shack, selling "jimmies"—heavy, fat, perfectly seasoned crabs—to tourists and locals alike.

Miss Shirley's Eastern Shore Crab Cakes

Almost fifty years later, that roadside crab shack has evolved into one of the largest seafood operations in America, Phillips Foods. Miss Shirley is still a part of the daily operation of her signature Ocean City restaurant, which serves thousands of crab cakes every season. According to Shirley, the secret to a good crab cake is good crab, lots of lumps, and simple seasoning.

Serves 6

2 eggs

2 teaspoons Worcestershire sauce

2 teaspoons lemon juice

2 teaspoons crab seasoning, such as Phillips' seafood seasoning (see Food Resource References, page 276)

2 teaspoons dried parsley flakes

2 heaping tablespoons mayonnaise

$1/2$ teaspoon dry mustard

2 heaping teaspoons prepared mustard

2 pounds jumbo lump crabmeat, picked over

4 slices white bread, crumbled

Vegetable oil, for frying

Soda crackers for serving

Tasty Tartar Sauce (recipe follows)

In a medium-size bowl, thoroughly combine the eggs, Worcestershire sauce, lemon juice, crab seasoning, parsley, mayonnaise, and mustards.

Place the crabmeat in a large bowl and gently fold in the breadcrumbs and the egg mixture so as not to break up the lumps. Shape into 12 slightly flattened balls and chill for at least 1 hour.

TO FRY THE CRAB CAKES: Pour oil into skillet to a depth of about $1^{1}/2$ inches. Heat the oil to 370°F and fry the crab cakes, a couple at a time, until golden brown, 4 to 5 minutes per side. Remove with a slotted spatula to paper towels to drain.

TO BROIL: Place crab cakes under a preheated broiler, turning to cook evenly, until nicely browned, 4 to 5 minutes per side.

Serve with soda crackers and Tasty Tartar Sauce.

Tasty Tartar Sauce

1 cup mayonnaise
1 tablespoon minced shallots
1/2 cup minced sour pickles,
    such as dill or cornichon
1 tablespoon sweet pickle
    relish, drained
1 teaspoon capers in vinegar,
    drained and chopped
Dash of lemon juice
1/2 teaspoon grated fresh or
    bottled horseradish, or to
    taste

Mix all the ingredients in a small bowl. Chill before serving.

CRAB OUT OF THE SHELL   Recipes calling for pounds of crabmeat require a picked and packed product. Dungeness crabmeat may be purchased fresh and frozen. The picked meat is a combination of lump, body meat, and legs and claws. Blue crabmeat, which is the most widely distributed, is a little more complex in types and grades. Let me explain.

Grades of Blue Crabmeat

JUMBO LUMP is the very best crabmeat that money can buy—all big pieces of sweet, succulent crab. To hold down your crab cake cost, mix jumbo lump with either lump or backfin.

LUMP contains some unbroken pieces of lump and whole body pieces. This is also an excellent product for crab cakes.

BACKFIN is a blend of meat from the entire body of the crab, which includes broken pieces of lump and pieces from the body of the crab.

SPECIAL indicates pieces of meat taken from the entire middle section of the body of the crab. This is good for casserole dishes and to extend crab cakes. Unless you purchase a pasteurized product, this type generally requires quite a bit of picking over for shells.

CLAW MEAT is the dark, sweet meat from the claws. Excellent for soups, stews, and chowders, it also makes a very good, low-cost crab cake.

CLAW FINGERS OR COCKTAIL CLAW are, once again, the darker meat, but in one whole piece with a small part of the tip of the claw attached, perfect for crab cocktails and dipping in sauces.

Fresh vs. Pasteurized vs. Frozen

FRESH

Obviously, in season, the best crabmeat to be had would be from local, fresh-picked crab. This is absolutely delicious and usually sold in one-pound containers. This type of crabmeat is highly perishable and only has a shelf life of several days.

PASTEURIZED

Pasteurized crabmeat has come a long way from the early days of pasteurizing and canning crab. An amazing new process, spearheaded by Phillips Foods, now provides outstanding picked crabmeat that holds its own right next to freshly picked—and it is available year round. Once pasteurized, the refrigerated product has a shelf life of twelve months. The great advantage to this product—in addition to its consistency and dependability—is that it is virtually shell-free, with just about no picking required, which saves valuable time.

FROZEN CRABMEAT

Frozen crabmeat would be my third choice. While still providing a nice crab flavor, the distinct, briny quality of the crab seems to "wash" away as the crabmeat defrosts. The frozen product has a higher moisture content, and therefore requires more breading to hold the meat together in recipes.

Mitchell Sjerven, owner of Bouchon in beautiful Santa Barbara, knows his way around a restaurant, having started out years ago in the business as a busboy. He is now at the helm of one of Southern California's most beloved dining establishments. Mitchell loves where he lives and this is reflected in his menu philosophy—the finest ingredients, prepared with care using an "as-fresh-and-as-local-as-possible" approach, with fish from the Santa Barbara Channel, and meats, poultry, and produce from the surrounding country-side.

Santa Barbara Crab Cakes

Serves 4

1 bunch green onions
4 tablespoons vegetable or olive oil, plus more for sautéing
1 fennel bulb, trimmed and diced
4 garlic cloves, sliced
1 red pepper, cut into medium dice
2 medium ears corn, kernels cut off cob
8 ounces fresh lump crabmeat
1 tablespoon whole-grain mustard
2 tablespoons toasted whole cumin seed (see note)
2 tablespoons chopped fresh thyme
2 tablespoons lime zest
1 whole egg, lightly beaten
4 tablespoons all-purpose flour
1 cup breadcrumbs
Salt and freshly ground black pepper
3 cups mesclun greens
Tomatillo and Lime Vinaigrette (recipe follows)

These California-style crab cakes can be made with West Coast Dungeness crab, or for a lumpier version, use lump blue crab. The vinaigrette makes a bit more than necessary for the dish, but is fantastic on all manner of salad and grilled fish. It will keep for a week in the refrigerator.

Trim the green onions. Dice the bottom white parts, and chop the green tops finely. Reserve in separate bowls.

Heat 4 tablespoons of oil in a skillet and sauté the fennel, garlic, green onion bottoms, red pepper, and corn until the fennel is soft.

In a large bowl, gently mix the crabmeat, mustard, cumin, green onion tops, thyme, lime zest, egg, flour, and breadcrumbs.

Combine the sautéed vegetables with the crab mixture and season to taste with salt and pepper. Adjust consistency, if needed, with more breadcrumbs.

Form mixture into cakes about $^1/_2$ inch thick by about 2 inches across.

Pour oil into a skillet to a depth of about $^1/_4$ inch. Heat the oil and fry the crab cakes, a few at a time, until golden brown,

about 3 minutes on each side. Remove with a slotted spatula to paper towels to drain.

Divide the mesclun greens among four plates and top with the crab cakes. Lightly drizzle some Tomatillo and Lime Vinaigrette over the lettuce and crab cakes. Serve at once.

Note: Put the cumin seeds in a dry skillet over medium heat and cook, shaking the pan so they don't stick, until fragrant, 1 to 2 minutes.

Tomatillo and Lime Vinaigrette

Makes about 1¾ cups

6 tomatillos, peeled and cored
3 garlic cloves
1 small white onion, diced
½ bunch cilantro, chopped
½ bunch green onions, green tops only, chopped
¼ cup champagne vinegar
2 tablespoons sugar
¼ cup lime juice
1 cup olive oil
Salt and freshly ground black pepper

Place tomatillos, garlic, and white onion in a saucepan. Add water to cover, bring to a boil, reduce heat, and simmer for about 35 minutes. Strain and discard liquid.

Place the tomatillo mixture in a food processor with the chopped cilantro and chopped green onion. Pulse to blend. Add vinegar, sugar, and lime juice and briefly process again. With the motor running, slowly add the olive oil and season with salt and pepper to taste.

Sitting in Mama Lan's San Francisco Bay kitchen and feasting on these stir-fried crabs, I was transported halfway around the world. Mama was one of my culinary mentors, a dear friend, and the finest seafood cook I have ever had the pleasure of working with.

Mama Lan's Vietnamese Stir-Fried Crab

This exotic dish is almost as much fun to make as it is to eat. And be sure to do as Mama did and serve plenty of steamed rice on the side, as well as slices of warm baguette to sop up the juices of the stir-fry. This is not a wine dinner—have plenty of cold beer on hand.

Mama Lan is no longer with us, but her family continues to prepare all her signature Vietnamese dishes at her namesake restaurant in Berkeley, California.

Serves 4

2 live Dungeness crabs (about 2½ to 3 pounds each)
Vegetable oil, for frying
2 cups all-purpose flour
Salt and freshly ground black pepper
6 tablespoons butter
6 tablespoons olive oil
3 stalks fresh lemongrass, grassy tops discarded and bulbs finely chopped
4 tablespoons minced garlic
2 tablespoons hot pepper flakes
3-inch piece fresh ginger, peeled and julienned
2 tablespoons tomato paste
3 tablespoons kosher salt
3 tablespoons sugar
1 bunch green onions, finely chopped
4 or 5 serrano chiles, sliced into thin rounds (optional) (see note)

Remove the top shell of the crab. Pull out the spongy gill and opaque matter in the center. Cut each crab into 4 pieces and with a mallet or edge of a knife make a crack (not all the way through) in each crab piece. This will allow the crab to absorb the cooking juices and make it easier to eat. In a large skillet or wok, pour in the vegetable oil until it reaches a depth of about 1 inch. Heat the oil and fry the top shells of the crab, turning, until crispy on both sides. Drain on a paper towel and set aside.

Season the flour with salt and pepper to taste. Dredge the crab pieces in the seasoned flour. Add the pieces to the hot oil and fry over fairly high heat, turning frequently, for 5 to 6 minutes. Remove to paper towels to drain and discard the cooking oil.

Place a large skillet or wok on medium heat and add the butter and olive oil. When the butter is melted, add the lemongrass, garlic, pepper flakes, and ginger and sauté for about 1 minute. (Mama's daughter, My Phuong, tells me that when you add the previous four ingredients they will start to "crackle" and they should be cooked until they stop crackling—which takes about 1 minute.) Add the tomato paste, mix well, and cook for 1 minute. Add the salt and sugar and simmer for 2 minutes. Add

the crab pieces (not the top shells) and stir, coating the crab pieces with the sauce. Cook, stirring often, for 4 to 5 minutes longer. Add the green onions and serrano chiles (if using) and remove from the heat.

For a beautiful presentation, arrange the crab pieces back in the shape of the crab. Divide three-quarters of the pan juices over each of the crabs. Then place the top shells back on the arranged crab pieces, pouring the remaining juices on top of the shells. Serve at once with plenty of napkins for messy hands. Mama would always supply a communal bowl of very warm water with several sliced lemon rounds and additional napkins when guests were nearing the end of their crab picking.

Note: Wear gloves when handling chiles and do not touch bare skin.

CRAB IN THE SHELL   Crabs—both blue and Dungeness—are sold whole, often live, or already cooked and ready to eat, but still in the shell. There are two major types of crab widely sold and readily available in the United States. Number one is the blue crab, which has the widest range, from the Mid-Atlantic to Florida and the Gulf of Mexico. Coming in at number two is the Dungeness crab, caught in Pacific waters and primarily available in northern California and the Pacific Northwest, though it may also be found in other major markets across the country. In addition there are the snow crab, local to the northern Pacific and northern Atlantic; the Jonah crab, from the northern Atlantic coast; the Alaskan king crab, from the icy waters of Alaska, sold frozen or previously frozen in the form of legs and claws; and the famous stone crab from Florida and the Keys—all of which are found in more select regional markets.

Til Purnell, of Sussex County, Delaware, says her version of this recipe begins, "First, catch your crabs." The recipe serves six as an entrée. Til says she has tried cutting the cakes in appetizer-size pieces, "but it's not very satisfactory—it just makes you hungry." Til, whose family was long established in Rehoboth Beach, Delaware, spent thirty-two years of her life overseas, mostly in Southeast Asia,

Til's Crab Foo Yong

where her husband worked in the Foreign Service. She often incorporates the cuisine of her youth with that of her adopted homes abroad.

Egg Foo Yong—the basis for this dish—has infinite variations of ingredients and seasonings, so feel free to experiment with cooked shrimp, scallops, or slices of grilled chicken breast in place of the crab. When making the egg mixture, add some chopped green onions and water chestnuts for color and texture. Instead of the cabbage, you can use bean sprouts or finely shredded Belgian endive or escarole—any crispy green that will cook through quickly.

Serves 6

8 eggs
1 small onion, finely chopped
1 cup finely shredded cabbage
1 teaspoon salt
1 pound fresh cooked crabmeat, preferably home-picked, shell and cartilage removed
4 tablespoons peanut or canola oil
Spicy Ginger Sauce (recipe follows)

Break the eggs into a large bowl and whisk until blended. Stir in the onion, cabbage, and salt; add the crabmeat and mix well.

Add the oil to a skillet and swirl pan to coat bottom and sides. Pour in the crab-egg mixture. Cook over medium heat until bottom is browned and mixture is nearly set. (If the bottom is browning too fast, turn down the heat.) Using two spatulas, turn the "omelet" over carefully and fry on the other side until lightly browned.

To serve, transfer to a platter and cut into 6 pieces. Top with Spicy Ginger Sauce and serve with white rice and Chinese vegetables.

Spicy Ginger Sauce

1 tablespoon soy sauce
1 tablespoon rice wine or dry
  sherry or dry white wine
1 tablespoon sugar
1 tablespoon grated ginger
2 tablespoons cornstarch

Put 1 1/2 cups water, the soy sauce, rice wine, sugar, and grated ginger in a small saucepan. Dissolve the cornstarch in the mixture and cook over medium-low heat until thickened, stirring occasionally.

STONE CRAB   Although harvested from the Carolinas to the Gulf, the legendary stone crab is most widely available in, and associated with, Florida. When the crabs are caught in traps along the coast and often out in the deeper waters of the Atlantic, one claw is snapped off and kept, while the crab itself is returned to the water, where it will regenerate a new claw. Talk about a renewable resource! The crab claws are cooked the same day either by the fisherman, or by one of the local processing houses. It seems that each fisherman has his own top-secret crabbing spot and top-secret recipe for the claws. The crab claws are sold fresh-cooked or frozen and graded as jumbo, large, select, and medium.

The high temple of stone crab, the world renowned Joe's Stone Crab in Miami Beach, Florida, is worth a special trip south, if you've never had the pleasure. The stone crab claws are served well chilled with a gigantic piece of meat exposed, just begging to be dipped in Joe's signature tangy mustard sauce. If you can't get to Joe's, try the spicy Three Mustard Sauce (page 99), or, for a different taste, a classic Remoulade Sauce (page 131).

Traditionally, this New Orleans dish was made with busters, the tiny soft-shell crabs that for conservation reasons are no longer harvested. But it's perfect made with any soft-shell crabs. Ask at the fish market for primes, jumbos, or hotels (see Grading Soft-Shell Crabs, page 120).

Béarnaise sauce, which is basically hollandaise with an herb reduction added, is lovely paired with sautéed soft-shelled crabs.

New Orleans Busters Béarnaise

Serves 4

1 cup all-purpose flour
1 teaspoon salt
$1/2$ teaspoon freshly ground black pepper
$1/4$ teaspoon cayenne pepper, or to taste
8 soft-shell crabs, primes or jumbos, cleaned (page 120)
4 tablespoons ($1/2$ stick) butter
2 tablespoons olive oil
Juice of 1 lemon
2 tablespoons chopped fresh parsley
Béarnaise Sauce (recipe follows)

In a medium bowl, stir together the flour, salt, pepper, and cayenne. Dredge the soft shells lightly in the flour mixture, shaking off the excess.

In a large skillet over medium-high heat, warm the butter and the oil. Add the crabs and sauté them for about 3 minutes on each side. Remove the cooked crabs to a heated platter and keep warm.

Pour off half the cooking oil and return the pan to the heat. Add the lemon juice and parsley. Heat for 1 minute, then pour over the crabs.

Serve crabs topped with a dollop of Béarnaise Sauce.

Béarnaise Sauce

3 tablespoons dry white wine
2 tablespoons white wine
    vinegar
1 tablespoon minced shallots
1 teaspoon minced fresh
    tarragon leaves
$1/4$ teaspoon freshly ground
    black pepper
$1/8$ teaspoon salt
3 egg yolks
2 tablespoons boiling water
8 tablespoons (1 stick) butter,
    melted
2 tablespoons chopped fresh
    parsley or tarragon leaves

In a small saucepan, combine the white wine, vinegar, shallots, tarragon, pepper, and salt. Bring to a boil and reduce to 1 tablespoon, 3 to 5 minutes. Set aside and allow to cool to room temperature.

In the top of a double boiler, or in a stainless steel mixing bowl, place the egg yolks, tarragon reduction, and the boiling water. Place over barely simmering water and whisk together until mixture becomes pale and creamy.

Remove from heat and gradually whisk in the melted butter to make a thick sauce. (The combination will work best if the butter and the egg mixture are the same temperature.) When thickened, gently whisk in the parsley or tarragon.

SOFT-SHELL CRABS   Most people I speak with are fairly confident that soft shells are a separate species of crab. But that's not the case. The type of soft-shell crabs that have become part of the American culinary landscape are blue crabs. That's it—just the feisty, ubiquitous scrapper that we know and love. Crabs, like all of us, need to grow, and the molting process is how they accomplish that. When the crabs make their way to the safety of the marsh grasses and back out of their shells, they are then in the "soft-shell" stage. A crab that lives out its entire three-year average life span may repeat this process up to twenty-two more times.

As soon as the crabs shed their shells, they need to be removed from the water and processed—either loaded into containers of hay and shipped live all across the country to the finest restaurants and seafood markets, or frozen.

Grading Soft-Shell Crabs

Whales—$5^1/_2$ inches and larger

Jumbos—5 to $5^1/_2$ inches

Primes—$4^1/_2$ to 5 inches

Hotels—4 to $4^1/_2$ inches

Cleaning Soft-Shell Crabs

Only soft-shell crabs that are alive need to be cleaned. If you purchase frozen soft-shells, the processor has already cleaned them and they are ready to use.

Rinse the crabs under cold water. With a pair of sharp scissors, cut off the eyes and mouth. This requires a cut straight across the face, about $^1/_4$ inch behind the eyes. Lift the pointed ends of the shell and snip out the spongy gills. Remove the apron from the underside of the crab, pulling away from the body (sort of like pulling up the tab on a can of soda or beer).

The crabs are now ready to use in your chosen recipe.

This recipe is from Shirley Phillips, the exuberant owner of Maryland's noted restaurant group and seafood supplier, Phillips Foods, of Baltimore. This lady knows her crabs. I love this recipe, because it is a novel variation of the traditional Shrimp Scampi, and because it's so quick and easy.

Phillips Crabmeat Scampi

Serves 4

4 tablespoons olive oil

4 tablespoons ($1/2$ stick) butter, cut into pieces

2 tablespoons chopped garlic

$1/2$ teaspoon dried red pepper

4 teaspoons Worcestershire sauce

2 tablespoons fresh lemon juice

$2/3$ cup white wine

1 pound jumbo lump crabmeat, picked over for shells

1 teaspoon chopped fresh parsley

Salt and freshly ground black pepper

1 pound cooked pasta, or 4 cups cooked rice

Heat the oil and butter in a large skillet over medium heat. Add the garlic and cook until garlic is lightly golden. Add the red pepper, Worcestershire sauce, lemon juice, and white wine. Bring to a boil and cook for 4 minutes. Gently stir in the crabmeat and parsley. Season with salt and pepper to taste. Serve over pasta or rice.

STEAMED BLUE CRABS These are my kind of crabs. The folks around the Chesapeake know of only one way to cook their crabs—and that would be steaming. Even the suggestion of boiling crab gets the blood rising. "You warsh away most of the good flavor, if you just stick 'em in a pot of boiling water," says Jackie Lee from Dorchester County, on Maryland's Eastern Shore. She has been picking crab since she was old enough to hold a knife and has eaten her fair share of the steamed variety. To be fair, I have had some wonderful crab that has been boiled, and it has to do with how the pot is seasoned. But for the old-fashioned flavor of a Chesapeake crab feast, this is how it's done.

Get out a big, heavy pot with a tight-fitting lid. Put a round rack in it and elevate it about 2 inches from the bottom of the pot. (Use heavy ceramic coffee cups or some other sturdy, heat-resistant cooking item.) Pour in one twelve-ounce can of beer (I use flat beer because it has a less metallic taste—see note following) and the same amount of white vinegar, and bring to a boil. Put in a layer of live hard-shell crabs and sprinkle them generously with Chesapeake seafood seasoning. Add another layer and more seafood seasoning and continue until all the crabs are in the pot with a good coating of seafood seasoning on top. Cover the pot and let it steam for twenty minutes. That's all there is to it. Put some newspapers on the table, set out some pitchers of ice-cold beer, dump the crabs out, and let the feast begin.

Note: To flatten beer, pour it into a bowl and let it sit for an hour or so.

For decades in the last half of the twentieth century, tourists, watermen, celebrities, and politicians streamed to tiny Smith Island in the center of the Chesapeake Bay. The draw was the inn run by Frances Kitching, legendary—and adamantly simple—arbiter of all things culinary around the bay. Mrs. Kitching, author of Mrs. Kitching's Smith Island Cookbook, *died in 2003, but her food traditions live on. This recipe is spiffed up a little for the twenty-first century, but it's still pretty basic, and allows the subtle flavor of the oysters to shine through.*

Smith Island Scalloped Oysters

Serves 4

4 tablespoons (1/2 stick) butter
1 package (about 40) unsalted soda crackers
1 pint oysters, with their liquor
1/4 cup grated onion (see note)
1/2 teaspoon salt
1/8 teaspoon freshly ground black pepper
1 tablespoon minced chives
Dash of Tabasco
1/2 teaspoon Worcestershire sauce
1/2 to 1 cup heavy cream

Preheat the oven to 350°F.

Liberally grease the bottom of a 1 1/2-quart casserole dish with 1 tablespoon of the butter.

Put about three-quarters of the crackers between sheets of wax paper and crush them with a rolling pin or the bottom of a skillet into fine crumbs.

Spread the crumbs evenly over the butter in the casserole. Spread the oysters on top of the crackers. Top with the grated onion and sprinkle with the salt and pepper.

Coarsely crumble the rest of the crackers with your fingers and mix these crumbs with the chives in a small bowl. Top the oyster layer with the chive-cracker mixture.

In the same small bowl, whisk the Tabasco, Worcestershire, and cream. Pour the cream mixture evenly over the dish. Bake for 30 to 40 minutes, or until top is golden.

Note: You can use a standard metal grater to grate the onion, but it's more comfortable to do it in an electric chopper or food processor.

Galveston, Texas, has been the home of the Gaido family for generations. They are with-out a doubt the first family of seafood in this Gulf Coast town, serving up local fare since 1911. Galveston Bay is teaming with American oyster varieties—Crassostrea virginica—that thrive in the bay and estu-aries behind the barrier islands separating the Texas mainland from the Gulf of Mexico.

Gaido's Baked Oysters Ponzini

These oysters are definitely a party favorite. The sauce can be made several hours ahead and then the dish popped in the oven just before serving. To prepare ahead of time, make sure the Ponzini sauce has cooled, and has been well chilled, before topping the oysters.

Serves 2 to 4

4 tablespoons extra virgin olive oil
1 small yellow onion, finely chopped
$\frac{1}{2}$ cup Chicken Stock (page 35)
$\frac{1}{2}$ pound mushrooms, finely chopped
1 cup heavy cream
$\frac{1}{4}$ cup dry white wine
$\frac{1}{2}$ teaspoon cayenne pepper
$\frac{1}{2}$ teaspoon salt
$\frac{1}{8}$ teaspoon nutmeg
$\frac{1}{2}$ pound Swiss cheese, coarsely grated
$1\frac{1}{4}$ cups grated Parmesan cheese
3 egg yolks
4 to 5 cups rock salt
2 dozen oysters on the half shell

Preheat the oven to 375°F.

Heat the olive oil in a large saucepan, sauté the onion over medium heat for 5 to 8 minutes, or until brown.

Add the chicken stock, mushrooms, cream, wine, cayenne, salt, and nutmeg to the saucepan. Bring almost to a boil. Turn off the heat.

Add the Swiss cheese, a little at a time, stirring constantly after each addition, until melted. Stir in the Parmesan cheese. Add the egg yolks and mix well. Cook over low heat, stirring con-stantly, until thickened.

Spread the rock salt $\frac{1}{4}$ to $\frac{1}{2}$ inch deep in a large baking pan. Nestle the oysters in the rock salt. Pour about 2 tablespoons of the sauce on top of each oyster. Bake for 15 minutes, or until the edges of the oysters curl.

GALVESTON, TEXAS

Galveston Island, Texas, is known for its gracious historic houses, its thirty-two miles of beaches, and its remarkable recovery from a devastating hurricane in 1900. But for a few years in the early nineteenth century, the island was known as the home of the notorious privateer Jean Lafitte. Lafitte presided over a little empire of boarding houses, pool halls, saloons, casinos, and a shipyard. He even had his own mansion, Maison Rouge. Lafitte was more interested in profit than politics, but he made a little mistake when he attacked an American ship and was forced to leave the island in 1821. It is said that he had a huge going-away bash, with boatloads of whiskey and wine for his pirates. They probably ate oysters, shrimp, and great big steaks. And when the party was over, he burned the settlement to the ground. Fortunately for Galveston, the party was only beginning.

ON THE HALF SHELL...OR NOT It looks oh so similar to a rock. It doesn't swim up or downstream, shed its shell, or even put up a good fight when yanked from the briny waters of its home. However, in vast numbers, these little creatures perform the powerful function of cleaning the waters of coastal estuaries and bays. They are oysters, the romanticized subject of poems and song, who've even had wars fought over them. Towns all around coastal America are built on their discarded shells.

While the oysters seem a timid lot, the fishermen who catch them are among the hardiest of seafaring souls. Oystering is regarded as the world's hardest, coldest work. The oysters themselves have mythic properties; among other things, they are said to be an aphrodisiac.

Oysters are sold in the shell by the dozen, or shucked in pints, quarts, and gallons. Shucked oysters are often gently simmered (don't overcook) in stews and chowders. They're also lightly fried, scalloped, steamed, and frittered. However, most oyster lovers look on those preparations with some element of disdain, knowing that the only civilized way to eat an oyster is raw.

Before the oyster is shucked, it should be well chilled and have a tightly closed shell. As soon as a sufficient number of oysters are shucked, they should be placed on a platter of ice, and served with a tangy cocktail sauce, or an herb-scented vinegar with a touch of minced shallots.

Oysters can be eaten raw on the half shell, barbecued, poached, steamed in spinach, and baked in the shell, but there is no finer eating than a perfectly fried oyster. Perfection is a crispy, not greasy, coating, with a plump briny oyster inside. Recipes run the gamut from frittered, to dusted just with flour, to this more southern-style mixture of cornmeal and flour, generously spiced. Remoulade is a classic French sauce, and whoever first developed the concoction must have had fried oysters in mind.

Southern Fried Oysters Remoulade

Serves 4

1 pint shucked oysters
1 cup finely ground yellow
   cornmeal
1 cup all-purpose flour
1 teaspoon salt
2 teaspoons Cajun seasoning
1 teaspoon freshly ground
   black pepper
$^{1}/_{2}$ teaspoon cayenne pepper
Vegetable oil, for frying
Remoulade Sauce (recipe
   follows)

Drain the oysters. Combine the cornmeal, flour, salt, Cajun seasoning, black pepper, and cayenne. Dust the oysters in the cornmeal-flour mixture, one at a time.

Pour oil into a frying pan to a depth of $1^{1}/_{2}$ inches and heat until quite hot, about 375°F. Add the oysters and fry for 4 to 5 minutes, or until golden brown. Do not overcrowd the skillet. Add more oil as needed. Remove the oysters with a slotted spoon or tongs to paper towels and drain well. Serve with Remoulade Sauce alongside for dipping.

Remoulade Sauce

1 cup mayonnaise

6 tablespoons finely minced celery

6 tablespoons finely minced green onion

3 tablespoons finely chopped parsley

1 teaspoon minced garlic

3 tablespoons prepared horseradish

2 tablespoons coarse-grain mustard

1 tablespoon chopped capers

3 tablespoons ketchup

2 tablespoons Worcestershire sauce

1 teaspoon Tabasco

1 teaspoon paprika

½ teaspoon salt

1 teaspoon finely minced anchovy (optional)

Mix all the ingredients together in a bowl. Cover several hours before serving.

QUICK AND EASY BBQ OYSTERS AND CLAMS   Want to impress your friends and keep them talking about what a great host you are? Get hold of a generous amount of oysters or clams, and just before the party, shuck them and place on a baking sheet, keeping them cold in the fridge. Have a bottle of your favorite BBQ sauce on hand (they'll never know you didn't make it). Top each piece of shellfish with about one tablespoon of sauce (depending on their size) and then about a one-inch piece of uncooked bacon. After your guests have their first drink, pop the baking sheet into a very hot (about 450°F) oven and bake for about eight minutes, or until the bacon begins to brown slightly. Transfer the oysters to a platter and serve at once.

Hard-shell clams are notoriously hard to open. Til Purnell, of Sussex County, Delaware, says she scrubs the clams thoroughly, and then puts them in a shallow container in the refrigerator for twenty-four hours. This causes them to open slightly. If you are extremely careful not to jostle them as you take them out, you can slip a knife in the slight opening, making the process much easier. But if you bump them at all, they'll snap shut again with a little hiss. Years ago, when Til served these to her prospective son-in-law, he asked if her daughter knew how to make the dish. When she said yes, he said, "I'll marry her on the spot."

Wedding Bell Clams

Serves 6

2 dozen hard-shell clams
1 large or 2 medium
    tomatoes, cored, seeded,
    and chopped
1 large green pepper,
    chopped
Salt and freshly ground black
    pepper
6 to 8 strips of bacon,
    quartered

Preheat the broiler.

Shuck the clams and separate the clams from their shells with a sharp knife, then leave them, with their liquor, on half of their shell. Check each shell and remove any grit or loose pieces of shell. Arrange the shells on a baking pan with a rim at least $^3/_4$ inches high, such as a jelly roll pan.

Mix together the chopped tomato and green pepper and season to taste with salt and pepper. Place some of the mixture on top of each clam. Place a strip of bacon on top of the tomato-pepper mixture and place the baking pan under the broiler until the bacon is crisp, 4 to 6 minutes. Watch to make sure the bacon doesn't burn. Serve immediately.

Stephen Garza is the "clam nanny" for many of south Florida's renowned chefs, such as Mark Militello, Michelle Bernstein, and Norman Van Aken. The Garza family's White Water Clams are farmed about 150 miles north of Miami on Sebastian Inlet in Pelican Island National Refuge, and distributed by the family's seafood outlet, Sun Ray Seafood. Customers rave about the clams' sweet, tender, and grit-free consistency. The carefully tended clam beds are technically "hard-shell clams"—or more formally Mercenaria mercenaria—but Stephen dubbed them "White Water" after the whitecaps that form on the inlet.

Sun Ray's White-Water Clams

Stephen reminds you to "be sure to have some Italian-style bread for dipping up all the great flavors of the broth." This garlicky tomato-and-bell-pepper wine sauce is easy to prepare, and you can use the same basic preparation with mussels.

Serves 2 to 4

24 hard-shell clams, or
    2 pounds of mussels
2 tablespoons extra virgin
    olive oil
2 tablespoons chopped garlic
1 small red bell pepper,
    julienned
1 small yellow bell pepper,
    julienned
$1/2$ cup white wine
1 medium tomato, cored and
    diced
$1/4$ cup chopped fresh basil
Freshly ground black pepper

Rinse the clams several times in cold water to remove loose grit.

Heat the olive oil in a large, heavy-bottomed saucepan. Add the garlic and bell peppers and cook over medium heat for several minutes, or until softened.

Raise heat to high and add the white wine. Bring to a full boil. Reduce heat and add the diced tomato. Simmer for 2 minutes.

Add the clams to the pot, increase heat, and cover tightly, steaming just until the clams open, 5 to 8 minutes. As the clams begin to open, sprinkle with the basil. Cover the pot and simmer for 1 minute longer.

Remove from the heat and add pepper to taste. Using a slotted spoon, remove clams from broth and arrange them neatly in a serving bowl. Carefully pour the steaming liquid over the top of the clams. Serve at once.

THE NEW ENGLAND CLAMBAKE

I'll be the first to admit it. I grew up on the Chesapeake Bay and we didn't have clambakes. However, I did live for a good bit of time on Cape Cod, and have attended my share. But I have never been the official "Bake Master," and that's where Ned Lightner, from Belfast, Maine, Clambake Master of the Universe, comes in to help us out. Ned has officiated at big clambakes for fifty to one hundred fifty people, though his start was fairly humble.

"There was this 'professional' guy—actually, the dad of one of my friends—who put on professional bakes on Cape Cod. He came to Bayside, Maine, which is right outside of Belfast, when I was about fifteen years old to make a special appearance. I was one of the kids enlisted to help in gathering rocks (he was very particular, wanting only granite rocks because they don't hold too much moisture—too much moisture and the rock can explode when it's being heated), seaweed—of which we needed lots, digging the fire pit, requiring good, old-fashioned hard work, and stacking the wood for the fire." After this, his first successful clambake, Ned hung up his clambake shovel for a while, resting on his teenage laurels.

Years later, when his local yacht club was trying to figure out how to raise money to start a sailing program for kids, Ned casually mentioned a clambake. He was declared Clambake Master on the spot.

"The first clambake was a big success, and I have put on at least one bake per summer for the past twenty years. I've attended some commercial bakes over the years but felt that they lacked the smoky flavor of the traditional bake, because they were basically steaming the food on a giant pan rather than over hot rocks." Authenticity doesn't come without a price. Ned says: "The method I use is a time-consuming and labor-intensive process, but it is pretty memorable and a local tradition." And it's the real thing!

All right, roll up your sleeves and take off your shoes. Here we go.

A Twelve-Step Clambake

1. Find a beach where cooking and open fires are allowed; if necessary, get a permit. It doesn't have to be an ocean beach, but if it is, that somehow makes the clambake taste better.

2. Gather friends and loved ones to dig. What is needed is a hole about one and one-half feet deep and four by five feet across.

3. Line the freshly dug hole with roundish rocks about eight to ten inches in diameter.

4. Build a fire. The idea here is to get the rocks hot, so the fire should be built in the middle of the hole with dry hardwood and maybe some very dry driftwood thrown in.

    Ned mixes his rocks and wood together so that the rocks heat more quickly. Once the fire is lit, it takes about three to three and a half hours to get the rocks good and hot. To check to see if the rocks are hot enough, spit on a rock (or for a more refined bake, drizzle on a little water), and it should sizzle.

5. When the rocks are hot-as-hell (white hot), rake and shovel out most of the wood and ashes and cover the rocks, now covering the bottom, with four to five inches of seaweed—we're talking a lobster sauna here.

6. Work fast now, and put down a layer of previously washed, tightly closed clams and another layer of seaweed.

7. Add a layer of live lobsters and another layer of seaweed.

8. Add a layer of small (new) potatoes and another layer of seaweed.

9. Add a layer of semi-husked corn (pull it down and remove the corn silk then pull husk back up around the ear of corn) and a final thick layer of seaweed.

10. Cover the hole with a wet canvas tarp, and if available an old sail (it looks good), and place heavy rocks around the edges of the tarp to hold it in place and keep the steam in while the clambake cooks.

11. Wait about one hour and fifteen minutes for everything to cook. Check near the end of the cooking time to test for doneness: Lobsters should be bright red, the potatoes easily pierced with a fork, and the clams open.

12. Remove the rocks and tarp and enjoy the clambake!!

NOTE: As a Clambake Master, Ned has developed some nifty techniques for feeding lots of people efficiently. He has wooden racks with openings in which he places lobsters, another for the potatoes and sausage, and yet another for veggies, corn, and whatever else he has come up with. He then puts these racks into the pit, with the hot rocks, covered with the seaweed, and when it is all finished cooking, he doesn't have to root through the seaweed to find all the food. When the bake is complete, he places the hot food in a bunch of coolers that he asks guests to bring (the coolers keep things hot as well as cold), and uses them to transport the food to where the tables are set and waiting for the feast. He also, some years back, procured a goodly number of cafeteria trays—you know, the bright red ones—and uses them as plates for the clambake.

Quantities for the clambake, per person

1 lobster, 1 to $1^1/2$ pounds
1 pound clams
1 pound mussels
1 ear corn
2 small potatoes
Optional:
Linguiça, chorizo, or other spicy sausage
Whole peeled onions
Whole heads of garlic

ACCOMPANIMENTS
Cold beer—Ned says any kind will do, but he enjoys a microbrewed
    pale ale
White wine for those so inclined
Sodas and iced tea
Melted butter
Lemons
Lobster bibs

DESSERT SUGGESTIONS
Cannon Beach Marionberry Cobbler (page 256)
Cold watermelon wedges

LOBSTER 101   The most familiar—as well as popular—lobster sold in the United States is from New England waters. To cook a lobster, fill a big pot about two-thirds full with generously salted water. When the water comes to a full rolling boil, place the lobster in the pot and cover with a tight-fitting lid.

Allow 15 minutes for a small 1 pounder
Allow 20 minutes for a medium $1^1/2$ to 2 pounder
Allow 35 to 40 minutes for the bigger guys ($2^1/4$ to 3 pounds)

Serve at once with bibs, lobster crackers to crack the claws, and plenty of melted butter. To use the meat in other recipes, allow the lobster to cool, and then spread the lobster out, flat on its back. First pull off the claws, separate the head from the tail section, and then run a sharp knife down the center length of the tail, but do not cut all the way through. Pull the shell apart and remove the meat. Crack the claws and remove the meat from them as well. The greenish part (tomalley) and the roe are both edible and considered fine eating by New Englanders. For a more extravagant, athletic, outdoor version, see The New England Clambake, page 136.

Those Portuguese really got around. Not only is their influence found in New England, but it's also found on the other side of the globe in tropical Hawaii. The Portuguese in New England were fishermen, while in Hawaii they were brought in to work on the planta-tions. Many of their culinary traditions still exist in the islands, as in this Asian-influenced Portuguese-style preparation.

Oahu Steamed Clams

Serves 6

3 tablespoons olive oil
1 large onion, chopped
2 tablespoons minced garlic
2 tablespoons minced ginger
1 medium red bell pepper, seeded and chopped
$1/2$ pound linguiça (Portuguese) sausage, diced (see note)
$1/2$ cup sake
3 cups Fish Stock (page 10)
2 cups clam juice
1 tablespoon Vietnamese chili-garlic sauce (tuong ot toi), or any chili paste
2 tomatoes, peeled, seeded, and diced (see note)
6 dozen clams, scrubbed
$1/2$ cup chopped fresh cilantro

Heat the oil in a large saucepan over medium-high heat and sauté the onion, garlic, ginger, and bell pepper for 2 to 3 minutes, or until the onions are translucent.

Add the sausage and sauté for 5 minutes more. Add the sake and stir, scraping up the browned bits from the pan. Add the fish stock and the clam juice and cook over medium heat for 12 minutes. Add the chili-garlic sauce, tomatoes, and clams.

Cover and cook until the clams open, 6 to 8 minutes. (Discard any that don't open.) Ladle the clams and broth into a bowl. Sprinkle with cilantro.

NOTES: If you can't find Portuguese sausage, use the more widely available Spanish chorizo.

To peel tomatoes, impale the tomatoes on the tines of a fork and immerse in boiling water for 10 seconds. The skin will pull off easily.

BASICALLY DELICIOUS STEAMED CLAMS OR MUSSELS   Steaming clams and mussels is basically a very simple process that can be elaborated upon endlessly—but let's keep it simple. This recipe works when steamed shellfish is called for in a recipe. It is also a delicious, easy way to make a big steaming bowl of shellfish for guests.

Allow approximately one pound of clams or mussels per person. Wash the shellfish well, and make sure that they are tightly closed. If they are slightly open, throw them out. Wild mussels will sometimes have a beard on the side that has to be pulled out.

In a pot large enough to easily hold all the clams or mussels you want to cook, pour in white wine to a depth of about one-eighth of an inch or so, and then an equal amount of cold water. (If there is no wine in the house, all water will work fine.) Put in the clams or mussels, cover the pot with a tight-fitting lid, and cook over high heat until they open. Keep an eye on them and don't overcook! As soon as the shells are opened, the clams or mussels are done.

Serve at once with melted butter and some of the cooking broth on the side. If using in a recipe calling for cooked shellfish, cool, and then proceed with the recipe instructions.

Food in Seattle is greatly influenced by Pacific Rim and Pan-Asian ingredients, and one of the chefs who pioneered this cuisine is Christine Neff. Chef Christine showcases her fusion cooking at her two highly popular restaurants, Flying Fish and Fandango.

Flying Fish Mussels with Chile-Lime Dipping Sauce

This recipe clearly shows its Asian influences in the use of ginger, lemongrass, and kaffir lime leaves. The first two have become fairly familiar to American cooks, but the third is less well known. Kaffir lime leaves are grown in Southeast Asia and Hawaii, are usually sold dried, and have a floral-citrus aroma. The best place to find them is in Asian markets and speciality food shops.

Serves 4 as an appetizer
2 pounds mussels
2-inch piece fresh ginger, peeled
$\frac{1}{2}$ stalk lemongrass (bottom half of stalk)
2 kaffir lime leaves (see note)
Chile-Lime Dipping Sauce (recipe follows)

Clean and debeard the mussels.

Cut the ginger and lemongrass on the bias, very thin. Cut the kaffir lime leaves into thin strips.

Place the mussels, ginger, lemongrass, lime leaves, and $1\frac{1}{2}$ cups water in a large shallow pot or wok and steam for 3 to 5 minutes, just until mussels start to open. (Discard any that don't open.)

Remove the mussels to a bowl and serve immediately with Chile-Lime Dipping Sauce.

NOTE: If kaffir lime leaves are not available, substitute 1 tablespoon lime zest.

Chile-Lime Dipping Sauce

8 Thai chiles (see note)
1/4 cup fresh lime juice
1/4 cup Vietnamese fish sauce
   (nuoc nam) (see note)
1 garlic clove, minced

Remove the chiles' stems and slice the chiles. Mix all the ingredients together and let set for 15 minutes before serving.

N O T E: If you can't find Thai chiles, substitute jalapeños. Wear gloves when handling chiles, and do not touch bare skin.

Vietnamese fish sauce can be found in Asian markets.

Rawle Jeffards, co-owner with his brother Ian, of Penn Cove Shellfish, is always knee-deep in mussels. On board their processing vessel, the Moule Mariner, *bobbing in the pristine waters surrounding Whidbey Island in Washington State, where these mussels are grown and harvested, the bivalves are cleaned, debearded, and then packed in mesh bags. As one would imagine, these guys know how to cook a batch of mussels properly.*

Mussels with Smoked Salmon and Cream

Serves 4

1 cup heavy cream
1/2 cup dry white wine
1 tablespoon chopped garlic
4 pounds mussels
3 ounces (1/3 cup) smoked
  salmon

Wood-smoked wild salmon, a staple of the Pacific Northwest, teams well with the mussels to produce this simple yet elegant dish. One of the wonderful aspects of cooking mussels in the finished sauce is that they produce a magnificent broth when they open, adding the finishing touch. Serve in bowls, with good bread for mopping up the sauce, or remove mussels from shells and serve over fettuccine.

Pour the cream and wine into a heavy-bottomed saucepan and add the garlic. Simmer over medium-high heat for 1 minute. Add the mussels and crumble in the smoked salmon. Cook over medium heat, stirring occasionally, uncovered, for 5 to 6 minutes, or until the mussels open and the meat is opaque. (Discard any mussels that don't open.) Do not allow liquid to boil, as the cream may curdle.

WHIDBEY ISLAND, WASHINGTON

Whidbey Island, a jewel in a setting of already gemlike beauty in the Pacific Northwest just north of Seattle, was shaped by the retreat 12,000 years ago of the Vashon Glacier. It's flat and fertile, the largest salt-water-surrounded island in the continental United States. There are two ferries to the mainland, but there's also a bridge at Deception Pass that was first conceived in the 1850s, but wasn't built until the 1930s.

The island has always been used for agriculture, first by the Marpole people, then by the Salish. Settler Isaac Ebey in the 1850s introduced potatoes, oats, pigs, and cattle. There's also a thriving fishing community and one of the Northwest's major purveyors of farmed shellfish, Penn Cove Shellfish. You may think you've never set eyes on Whidbey Island, but if you're a movie buff, you saw it in *Practical Magic, Double Jeopardy,* and *Snow Falling on Cedars.* It's not a big place (just over 208 square miles), but it's a big star.

Whidbey Island, Washington, mussel farmer Tim Jones, of Penn Cove Shellfish, spends his days on the water checking the growth rate and expected harvest time for his brood of pearly black mussels. You might think it would be a busman's holiday to want to indulge in an end-of-the-day meal of plump mussels, but you would be mistaken, because Tim likes nothing better than to partake of the fruits of his labor.

Marinated Penn Cove Mussels

Serves 5 to 6

5 cups rice wine vinegar
2 cups sugar
$\frac{1}{2}$ cup finely diced red
    pepper
$\frac{1}{3}$ cup finely diced daikon
    (see note)
3 green onions, finely sliced
3 tablespoons finely chopped
    parsley
1 tablespoon finely diced
    fresh ginger
2 tablespoons sesame oil
5 pounds steamed mussels
    (still in shell), cooled
    (see Basically Delicious
    Steamed Clams or
    Mussels, page 143)

Fishermen making this dish would normally put a little salted water in a pot, bring it to a boil, pile in the washed and debearded mussels, put on a lid, and let them quickly steam just until the shells opened. That method will work fine here, but I have also referenced a recipe for steamed garlic mussels. By preparing them with garlic and aromatic vegetables, the meat of the mussels will be more flavorful. Either way, this is a fine kettle of mussels. They are prepared ahead and chilled. Serve as a summer appetizer or as a light meal with a green salad and crusty bread.

Combine the vinegar, sugar, red pepper, daikon, green onions, parsley, ginger, and sesame oil in a large glass or ceramic bowl. Add the mussels and gently toss to coat well. Let marinate in the refrigerator for 2 to 3 hours, gently tossing from time to time before serving.

NOTE: Daikon is a Japanese or Chinese radish. If you can't find it in your local supermarket, try a Japanese or Chinese speciality shop.

Kings of tailgate, high-fat, and even-higher-cholesterol cuisine, the Feasty Boys are hosts of a down-home, no-holds-barred cable cooking show. Both Feastys are definitely at home in the kitchen. Feasty Jon spent much of his formative years working in restaurants and is still in the food business. Feasty Jim trained as a U.S. Coast Guard chef and landed a tour of duty on the USCG tall ship, the Eagle, serving as the captain's personal chef—now that's coastal cooking! The Feastys put their own spin on this nineteenth-century sandwich out of New Orleans. Legend has it that when the gentlemen of New Orleans spent a night carousing in the French Quarter, they would bring their frying pan–wielding wives one of these sandwiches as a sort of "peace offering," so to speak.

Feasty "Peacemaker" Sandwich

Serves 4

1 loaf Italian bread
6 tablespoons butter, softened
$1/2$ cup shredded Romano cheese
$1/2$ pound bacon
2 cups all-purpose flour
$1/2$ teaspoon salt
2 teaspoons Cajun or seafood seasoning
$1/2$ teaspoon freshly ground black pepper
1 pint shucked oysters
2 tomatoes, cored and thickly sliced
1 pint sour cream
2 teaspoons prepared horseradish
Salt, for seasoning

Preheat the oven to 375°F. Cut the top third (lengthwise) off the Italian bread loaf. Remove most of the inside of the bottom of the bread, creating a bowl-like effect. Spread the butter on the inside and the top of the loaf and place them separately on a baking sheet. Bake for 6 to 7 minutes, or until the bread becomes crisp and somewhat toasted. Remove from the oven and sprinkle the bottom of the loaf with the Romano cheese.

In a skillet, fry the bacon, reserving the bacon grease, and drain the bacon on paper towels. Coarsely chop the bacon and set aside.

Combine the flour, salt, Cajun seasoning, and black pepper on a plate and mix well. Dredge the oysters in the seasoned flour.

Heat the skillet with the reserved bacon grease and when the grease is hot, fry the oysters for about 2 to 3 minutes per side, or until nicely browned. As the oysters are finished, put them into the cheese-lined bread loaf.

Fry the sliced tomatoes in the remaining bacon grease for several minutes. While the tomatoes are cooking, combine the sour cream and horseradish. Spoon it liberally over the oysters. Sprinkle the chopped bacon over the oysters and horseradish sauce inside the loaf. Top off with the fried tomatoes, sprinkle with salt and pepper, replace the top of the loaf, and DIG IN!

On the Chesapeake where I grew up, in whatever direction one turns, a crab house is always steaming huge kettles of blue crabs, permeating the air with the wafting aromas of the bay's ubiquitous regional seasoning.

Old Bay Shrimp Fest

A heavy, steamed jumbo blue crab encrusted with spicy Old Bay is a joy unto itself, but for a great no-muss-no-fuss backyard get-together, this shrimp fest cannot be beat. It's a one-pot meal, cooked in layers, beginning with ingredients that take the longest to cook and ending up with the succulent jumbo shrimp on top. Serve with plenty of cold beer and maybe some ginger beer for the kids. If I am hosting this fest in the dog days of summer, I always serve some ice-cold watermelon to complete the occasion.

Serves 8

1/2 cup Old Bay seasoning
2 tablespoons salt
1 can (12 ounces) beer
8 medium red potatoes, cut into quarters
2 large sweet onions, cut into wedges
2 pounds lean smoked sausage, such as chicken or turkey, cut into 2-inch lengths
8 ears fresh corn, shucked, broken in half
4 pounds large shrimp

In an 8-quart stock pot, bring the Old Bay, salt, 4 quarts of water, and beer to a boil. Add the potatoes and onions; cook over high heat for 8 minutes. Add the smoked sausage to the pot; continue to cook on high for 5 minutes. Add the corn; continue to boil for 7 minutes. Add the shrimp in their shells; cook for 4 minutes.

Drain the cooking liquid and pour the contents of the pot into several large bowls, shallow pails, or simply mound on a paper-covered picnic table. Sprinkle with additional Old Bay if desired.

SHRIMP   Most shrimp are caught far out at sea and frozen instantly. Unless you live near a shrimpers' port, shrimp you'll find in your market are usually sold as "previously frozen." Thaw them in the refrigerator before cooking.

At least twenty different kinds of shrimp show up in U.S. markets, and they come in all sizes. Shrimp are sold by "count," that is, by about how many of them will weigh one pound. A pound of the tiniest shrimp will contain 150 to 180; a pound of "colossal" will contain only about ten. The lower the count, the higher the price.

Shrimp are second only to tuna in popularity in the United States, and with good reason: They can be boiled or broiled, sautéed or poached, baked or steamed, microwaved or stir-fried. Their mild flavor makes them excellent companions to all kinds of other foods, from grits and gravy to the Creole seasonings of onion, celery, green peppers, tomatoes and Tabasco—definitely a food it's hard to eat one of!

For some folks, grits connote "southern" or "soul food," but to Doretha Lee of Charleston, South Carolina, who has worked in the seafood business "since I was tall enough to reach the work counter," grits just mean good home cooking. Cornmeal and shrimp have always been plentiful and a staple in many homes along the southern Atlantic coast. Miss Doretha delights her guests with this sophisticated version of the old standard, grits and gravy.

Cheese and Garlic Grits with Shrimp and Tasso Gravy

Serves 4

1 cup quick grits
8 tablespoons (1 stick) butter
1 cup sharp cheddar cheese, cubed
2 garlic cloves, minced
1 egg
$^1/_2$ to $^3/_4$ cup milk
Salt and white pepper
2 bay leaves
16 jumbo headless shrimp
Tasso Gravy (recipe follows)

Prepare the grits according to package directions.

When the grits are cooked, stir in the butter, cheese, and garlic.

Break the egg into a 1-cup mixing cup and whisk slightly. Add enough milk to make 1 cup liquid, mix, and stir into the grits mixture. Season to taste with salt and white pepper.

In a large saucepan, combine 2 quarts of water with 1 tablespoon salt and the bay leaves. Bring to a boil. Reduce heat until water is boiling gently and add the shrimp. Cook just until the shrimp are done, 3 to 5 minutes, then drain them in a colander. When the shrimp are cool enough to handle, remove their shells (leaving tail), and devein, if desired.

To serve, place the grits in the middle of 4 plates. Spoon or drizzle the Tasso Gravy over the grits, then place 4 shrimp on top.

Tasso Gravy

2 tablespoons salted butter
1/4 cup thinly sliced and
    finely chopped tasso
1/4 cup all-purpose flour
2 cups Chicken Stock (page
    35)
Salt and white pepper

Tasso, which is a highly seasoned, smoked, Cajun-style, cured pork shoulder, adds a remarkably flavorful dimension to the dish. Outside the South, tasso can be found in specialty shops. (See page 276.)

In a small saucepan, melt the butter over low heat. Add the tasso and sauté until slightly browned, about 3 minutes. Stir in the flour to make a roux. Sauté for 3 more minutes, then add the chicken stock 1 cup at a time, stirring until well blended. Simmer for 15 minutes. Season to taste with salt and white pepper.

George "Paw Paw" Davis makes his home on the Magothy River, just north of Annapolis, Maryland. I've had shrimp—both steamed and boiled—on the Atlantic, Pacific, and Gulf coasts, and all I can tell you is this: Nobody does it better than Paw Paw.

Paw Paw's Windmill Point Peel 'n' Eat Shrimp

He says to file this recipe under A for attitude, because that's what you need when you make it. He will not even acknowledge the possibility that anyone would make this feast with less than five pounds of jumbo shrimp. He says, "Not worth getting yourself worked up for any less." It would be sacrilegious at the Davis homestead to have a Sunday afternoon football party without these shrimp. They make the game.

Serves a crowd
(10 to 15 people)

Two 12-ounce bottles
domestic beer

1 1/2 cups Chesapeake seafood
seasoning

5 pounds jumbo shrimp
(15-to-20-count size is
good), shell on

Windmill Point Cocktail
Sauce (recipe follows)

I think Paw Paw tells it best here. "Get a big old pot, maybe like a stock pot or steamer pot with a steaming basket that fits into it and a good tight-fitting lid. Pour the beer into the pot and add about 1/2 cup Chesapeake seafood seasoning; don't be shy. Add water to the pot to bring the liquid level up to the bottom of the steaming basket. The trick is you want enough liquid, but don't want the shrimp sitting in it.

"Place half of the shrimp in a large bowl and pour in a half cup of seafood seasoning and mix well. Put the seasoned shrimp into the steaming basket, and when the stockpot is screaming-steaming, place the basket into the pot and cover with the lid.

"The name of the game here is 7 minutes. You want to stir up the shrimp about every 2 minutes.

"Halfway through the cooking time, at about 7 minutes, do the taste test. The shrimp should be cooked through, with crisp shells—you don't want them soggy, and overcooking or letting them sit in the liquid will do just that. If the shrimp are not quite done, give them about 2 minutes more.

"Dump the shrimp into a bowl and put it out with plenty of cocktail sauce for dipping.

"Season the second half of the shrimp with a half cup of seafood seasoning and repeat the cooking process. You can use the same steaming liquid that you steamed the first batch with, adding a little more water if necessary."

Paw Paw's Windmill Point Rule Number 1—Do not peel the shrimp! The shell is the natural wrapper, and it keeps them crisp and moist inside.

Rule Number 2—Do not peel shrimp for anybody. They need to do it themselves to get the seasoning on their fingers while they're eating the shrimp. That's what makes it taste so good.

Windmill Point Cocktail Sauce

2 cups ketchup
2/3 cup prepared horseradish
Juice of 2 lemons
1 teaspoon Tabasco

Combine all the ingredients in a bowl and mix well.

Creole-style cooking comes from the French and Spanish who made their home in New Orleans and along the Louisiana coast, and like Cajun cooking, makes maximum use of the cooking "trinity"—green bell peppers, celery, and onions. Leroy "Otz" Sullivan moved to Punta Gorda, Florida, quite a number of years ago when it was a much smaller town. He made friends with a band of fishermen, and in season had piles of fresh shrimp at his disposal—and he made good use of them, as this Creole sauce will attest. Leroy says to "brown the onions real good—makes 'em sweet. But if ya let 'em go too long they'll burn on ya. And then you'll have to throw 'em out, or the sauce will be bitter as gall."

Leroy's Punta Gorda Shrimp Creole

This recipe makes a fine accompaniment to Pan-Fried Catfish with Shrimp Creole Sauce (page 96), or to just about any fried or grilled, firm, meaty fish. Although it is not in the original recipe, I throw in a generous pinch of sugar (about a teaspoon) while the sauce is simmering, as it takes out some of the acidity of the tomatoes. Time permitting, it is a good idea to make the sauce a day ahead and then cook the shrimp in the Creole Sauce just before serving. Traditionally, this meal is served with or on rice.

Serves 4 to 6

5 tablespoons olive or vegetable oil
2 cups finely diced onions
1 1/2 cups finely diced celery
1 1/2 cups finely chopped green onions
1 1/2 cups finely diced green bell peppers
2 tablespoons minced garlic
3/4 teaspoon cayenne pepper
1 1/2 teaspoons salt
1/2 teaspoon freshly ground black pepper
1/2 teaspoon fennel seeds
1 teaspoon Tabasco
1 1/2 teaspoons dried basil
1 1/2 teaspoons dried thyme
2 bay leaves
2 cups Fish Stock (page 10), (see note)
1 teaspoon sugar, optional
3 cups tomatoes, peeled and chopped, fresh or canned
2 tablespoons tomato paste
1 1/2 pounds shrimp, peeled and deveined (reserve shells)

Heat the oil in a saucepan over medium heat and add the onions, cooking and stirring frequently for 8 to 10 minutes, or until nicely browned (see Leroy's admonishment above). Add the celery, green onions, and bell peppers and cook for 5 minutes more. Add the garlic, cayenne, salt, pepper, fennel, Tabasco, basil, and thyme and cook for 3 minutes.

Add the bay leaves, fish stock, sugar, if using, tomatoes, tomato paste, and 1/2 cup water.

Bring the mixture almost to the boil, then reduce the heat and let the sauce slowly cook for 1 hour, stirring occasionally. The sauce can be prepared ahead to this point and refrigerated, then reheated shortly before cooking the shrimp.

Before serving, reheat the Creole sauce and add the shrimp, cooking for 5 to 6 minutes, or until the shrimp are cooked through and no longer translucent.

NOTE: If you are making the Fish Stock just for this recipe, add the shrimp shells to the stock. If you already have stock on hand, add some shrimp shells to it and simmer for 15 minutes, straining out the shells before using in the Creole sauce. If you really want to make this dish, but have neither the ingredients nor the will to make a fish stock, don't despair—just simmer the peeled shrimp shells with about $2^1/2$ cups water before preparing the Creole.

I don't believe one could find a more spectacular location for a restaurant than the Portola Café's dining room at the Monterey Bay Aquarium. Floor-to-ceiling windows overlook a breathtaking view of Monterey Bay and the California coast. The innovative menu, by chef Tim Fisher, is another surprise for a first-time visitor. The café creates light, California-inspired dishes, many of which are composed of seafood. But the Portola Café serves only sustainable seafood items as recommended by the aquarium's Seafood Watch program.

The key to preparing this unbelievably delicious recipe is to have everything done ahead of time. Do all of your prep for the sauté first, then prepare the polenta. I promise you it is well worth the effort, and you will feel every bit the pro when you serve your guests.

Seared Scallops with Orange, Fennel, and Polenta

Serves 4

¼ cup olive oil
24 large dry-pack sea scallops (see note)
2 shallots, diced
1 tablespoon finely chopped fresh ginger
2 garlic cloves, sliced
2 heads fennel, core removed, julienned
¼ cup dry white wine
½ cup fresh orange juice
Salt and freshly ground black pepper
3 tablespoons butter
3 oranges, sectioned, pith removed
Parmesan Polenta (recipe follows)

Heat the olive oil in a large skillet over high heat and sear the scallops for about 3 to 4 minutes on each side, until light brown. The scallops should be medium-rare. Set aside.

Drain excess oil from the pan, add the shallots and sauté until tender and brown. Add the ginger, garlic, and fennel and toss lightly. Add the wine and continue cooking until the fennel is tender, and the wine is almost completely reduced, about 5 minutes. Add the orange juice and salt and pepper to taste.

When the orange juice comes to a boil, whip in the butter and remove from heat. Add the orange sections.

To serve, place the polenta in the center of a plate, arrange the scallops around the polenta, and spoon the fennel-orange sauce over.

NOTE: Some scallops are packaged with water, while others are packed without extra liquid. In a recipe that calls for searing, the dry-packed scallops work better.

Parmesan Polenta

1/2 teaspoons salt
1/2 cup polenta
2 tablespoons butter
3 tablespoons Parmesan
  cheese
Salt and freshly ground black
  pepper

Bring 3 cups of water to a boil in a heavy saucepan. Add the salt, then slowly add the polenta stirring constantly with a wire whisk. Lower heat to a simmer and cook the polenta until thick and shiny, 15 to 20 minutes. Add the butter, cheese, and salt and pepper to taste. Cover to keep warm while preparing the scallops.

Étouffée means "smothered." And that is exactly what happens to the shellfish in this dish, which are smothered in a thick, spicy array of vegetables and seasonings, and, as with most other southern coastal dishes, eaten with an ample serving of rice.

Crawfish Étouffée

Crawfish are available fresh in parts of the South, and can be found frozen in other parts of the country. If you can't find crawfish, use shrimp. Best if made ahead, up to several days, and reheated before serving, this Cajun classic goes well with South of the Mason-Dixon Line Cornbread (page 230).

Serves 8

$^1/_2$ cup vegetable oil
$^2/_3$ cup all-purpose flour
$^1/_2$ cup minced onions
$^1/_2$ cup minced celery
$^1/_2$ cup minced green bell
 pepper
2 tablespoons minced garlic
$3^1/_2$ cups Fish Stock (page 10)
2 teaspoons salt
1 teaspoon cayenne pepper
2 teaspoons freshly ground
 black pepper
1 teaspoon dried basil
1 teaspoon dried thyme
8 tablespoons (1 stick) butter
1 cup chopped green onions
2 pounds crawfish tails,
 cleaned

Pour the vegetable oil into a cast-iron skillet and heat until very hot, nearly smoking. Whisk in the flour, a bit at a time, and cook, whisking constantly, until the mixture is a dark red-brown, about 5 minutes. Keep the mixture moving in the skillet; do not let it scorch. (Also be careful not to get it on your skin, as it is very hot.)

When the desired color is reached, take the skillet off the heat and stir in the onions, celery, bell pepper, and garlic. Sauté, still off heat, until the vegetables are limp, about 5 minutes. Set aside.

Put the fish stock into a large saucepan and bring to a boil. Gradually add the roux mixture, whisking constantly, until all is incorporated and the mixture is thickening. Stir in the salt, cayenne pepper, black pepper, basil, and thyme.

Melt the butter in a heavy skillet or pot large enough to hold all the crawfish. Add the green onions and crawfish and sauté until crawfish are cooked through, 5 to 8 minutes.

Stir the crawfish mixture into the stock mixture, and let sit at least 15 minutes before serving. Preferably, let it cool in the pot, then store in the refrigerator for several hours or up to 2 to 3 days.

CRAWDADDY BOIL Folks generally associate crawfish or crayfish or crawdaddys—you choose—with Louisiana, but they actually can be found all over the United States. I remember as a kid watching them walk along the bottom of our neighborhood creek, but had not an inkling that they could be a delicious food. However, they did figure it out down in Louisiana Cajun country, where it is definitely "crawfish," and sometimes "crawdads." The crawfish are prepared in many composed dishes, but the all-time favorite recipe is the time-honored crawfish boil.

The preparation is true to the name, but as one would imagine, down in the Cajun world, they spice things up a tad. We'll figure that we're boiling for six people. I always plan on one pound live crawfish per person, so you do the math. First soak the crawfish in cold water, changing the water a number of times to get out any muddiness they may have brought along with them.

In a lobster pot or stock pot, bring a couple of gallons of water to a boil. While the water is heating, add about one cup salt, a few lemons cut into slices, six onions cut into quarters, six small "new" potatoes cut in half, four stalks of chopped celery, six bay leaves, a pinch of thyme leaves, and a generous teaspoon of cayenne pepper. Now throw in three bags of crab boil—a secret blend of Louisiana ingredients (page 275). Bring the whole shebang to a boil and let it rip for around twelve minutes.

Now it's time for the crawdads. Put them in the pot, and give them a stir. If it seems too crowded in there, add a little more water to the pot. Return it all to a boil and cook for another ten minutes. Remove the crawfish and vegetables with a slotted spoon onto a serving platter or large bowl.

Serve warm, but if—and it's not likely—there are any crawdads left over, they are great eaten cold later. Serve the Crawdaddy Boil with plenty of cold beer.

Puffy Conch Fritters

Steve Garza, of C Farms, in Miami Lakes, Florida, wants the whole world to appreciate conch. He is a man on a mission and raises the beautiful-shelled conch at Caicos Conch Farm, on the Turks and Caicos Islands. Steve distributes conch fresh to chefs and seafood markets all over the country, and says that the fresh version is very tender and needs only brief cooking and no pounding to tenderize.

One of Floridians' favorite snacks are these puffy conch-filled fritters. There are as many conch fritter recipes floating around the Citrus State as there are crab cake recipes up in my neck of the woods. This rendition produces spicy little devils depending on the ferocity of the peppers used. The Scotch bonnet peppers are hot, so plan accordingly.

Makes about 24 small fritters

2 cups all-purpose flour
2 teaspoons baking powder
1 teaspoon sea salt
$1/4$ teaspoon freshly ground black pepper
3 eggs, lightly beaten
$3/4$ to 1 cup milk
$1/4$ cup finely diced yellow bell pepper
$1/4$ cup finely diced green pepper
$1/4$ cup finely diced red pepper
$1/4$ cup finely diced white onion
1 Scotch bonnet pepper, finely diced (see note), or other hot pepper such as serrano
1 pound finely chopped conch (see Food Resource References, page 275)
Vegetable oil for frying
Spicy Orange-Dijon Sauce (recipe follows)

Mix together the flour, baking powder, salt, and pepper in a large bowl. In a small bowl, mix together the eggs and milk. Beat the egg mixture into the dry ingredients until a smooth batter is formed. Add the remaining ingredients, except for vegetable oil and sauce, and mix well.

Pour oil into a skillet to a depth of 1 to $1^1/2$ inches and heat until very hot, about 375°F. Drop the batter in by the tablespoonful, or a very small scoop, 3 to 4 fritters at a time, being sure not to crowd them together, and fry until golden brown, 2 to 3 minutes. Remove with a slotted spoon to paper towels to drain. Serve with Spicy Orange-Dijon Sauce.

NOTE: As always when working with hot peppers, wear gloves and don't touch bare skin.

Spicy Orange-Dijon Sauce

Juice of 2 oranges
$^1/_3$ cup Dijon mustard
1 teaspoon honey
2 tablespoons seeded and
　　minced Scotch bonnet
　　pepper (see note)
$^1/_2$ cup sweet relish

Mix all the ingredients together.

NOTE: Wear gloves when handling chiles and do not touch bare skin. Scotch bonnet peppers are among the hottest of hot peppers. Reduce amount to make a milder sauce.

PREPARING CONCH Most conch found in the United States is frozen. Conch can be tough, so it needs to be prepared and cooked properly. First trim off any pieces of dark membrane. Then place the conch between two pieces of plastic wrap and pound it with a ridged mallet until it is less than one-quarter of an inch thick. Conch are most tender when lightly cooked (simmered in salted water or vegetable stock for 5 minutes), or when cooked for a longer time, 30 to 40 minutes. For fritters and stews, chop the conch in a food processor or use a meat grinder.

Coastal is our theme, but this book is not just about seafood and shellfish. The coastal communities of the United States are rich with recipes from the land as well. Early settlers arriving on the coasts brought chickens, cattle, goats, and pigs with them and found abundant native game: deer and elk, ducks and turkeys, buffalo, rabbits, squirrels, and 'possums. Later waves of immigra-

5 POULTRY AND MEAT

tion brought new ingredients and preparations, a bit of jazz alongside the classic, traditional methods.

The variations of meat, poultry, and game recipes can be limitless. After all, we're talking about things that can be baked, boiled, broiled, braised, roasted, pan-fried, deep-fried, stir-fried, fricasseed, stewed, steamed, sautéed, grilled, seared, slow-cooked, barbecued, marinated, dry-rubbed—you get the picture. And, preparation aside, there's no spice, herb, vegetable, fruit, nut, grain, starch, or condiment that can't be used to enhance these foods.

These recipes include a mix of the very traditional and the purely modern, the down-home and the haute. From pork chops to duck breast or a fabulous oxtail braise, these recipes speak clearly of their regional origins.

Sounds like a French-Cuban dish, does it not? Well, not actually. Versailles is the ever-popular Cuban restaurant in Miami's Little Havana with a very French-sounding name. When Felipe Valls Sr. originally opened his small family restaurant in 1971, he decided on a décor reminiscent of a French palace. But this is not a tourist restaurant. It is the real deal, with multiple generations of expatriate Cubans jamming the tables and discussing local events, and the cuisine remains true to Señor Valls's Cuban roots.

Versailles Cuban Chicken with Rice

Here we have Versailles's most popular dish, Arroz con Pollo à la Cubano, in a recipe from chef Tony Piedra. Cuban food has its origins in traditional Spanish food and is not, as many assume, a spicy cuisine. This comforting dish is typical. With the addition of cerveza (beer) at the finish, it becomes the Cuban version of "drunken chicken." Serve with fried plantains and a simple salad of avocado, onion, and tomato.

Serves 4

One 3- to 3$\frac{1}{2}$-pound chicken, cut into 8 pieces
Salt and freshly ground black pepper, for seasoning
$\frac{1}{2}$ cup extra virgin olive oil
1 large onion, finely chopped
1 garlic clove, finely chopped
1 medium green bell pepper, diced
$\frac{1}{2}$ cup tomato sauce
$\frac{1}{2}$ cup white wine
5 cups Chicken Stock (page 35), heated
2 cups arborio rice
1 teaspoon salt
$\frac{1}{2}$ teaspoon freshly ground black pepper
12 ounces (1 can) domestic beer, at room temperature
$\frac{1}{2}$ cup pimientos, cut in thin strips, for garnish
$\frac{1}{2}$ cup petite peas, fresh or frozen, briefly blanched and cooled, for garnish

Preheat the oven to 375°F.

Generously season the chicken pieces with salt and pepper. Put the oil in a stovetop, ovenproof casserole or Dutch oven over medium-high heat. Add the chicken and brown on both sides, until golden brown, 5 to 6 minutes.

Add the onion, garlic, and green pepper and sauté for 5 minutes over medium heat. Add the tomato sauce, white wine, and hot chicken stock. Bring the liquid to a boil and add the rice, the teaspoon of salt and the $\frac{1}{2}$ teaspoon of pepper.

Reduce the heat and simmer for 20 minutes, stirring gently. Cover and finish in the oven. The rice should be tender and the chicken should be cooked through, so juices run clear when pricked with a knife, about 30 minutes. Remove from the oven; pour the beer over the casserole and garnish with pimientos and peas.

MIAMI, FLORIDA

What people think of as "Miami" is actually two places: the city of Miami, which is on the mainland, wedged between Miami Bay and the Everglades, where all the tall buildings are; and the city of Miami Beach, which is on a barrier island about two miles offshore. Miami Beach is home to South Beach, the outrageously trendy neighborhood of clubs and restaurants featured in the Robin Williams–Nathan Lane movie *The Birdcage,* and to the Art Deco National Historic District, a mile-square area that contains possibly the largest collection of 1920s through 1940s Deco-style architecture anywhere. Both cities are noted for their food and nightlife and the influence on their culture of Latin immigrants. Both places are mere youngsters on the East Coast. Miami was incorporated in 1892, and Miami Beach development began around 1913.

This is a traditional Hawaiian dish. It's said there are as many versions of this recipe as there are households cooking it, so feel free to add or subtract ingredients, or to alter the spices. The "rice" is actually extra-thin rice-flour noodles, broken into small pieces.

Big Island Chicken Long Rice

Place the noodles in a bowl and add warm water to cover. Soak for 1 hour.

Serves 4

8 ounces Chinese rice
   noodles, broken into 2- to
   3-inch lengths
4 cups Chicken Stock (page
   35)
One 2^1/2- to 3-pound chicken,
   cut into pieces
1-inch piece of ginger, peeled
   and crushed
2 tomatoes, peeled, seeded,
   and chopped (see note), or
   one 14-ounce can diced
   tomatoes
1 large carrot, julienned
2 celery stalks, thinly sliced
2 to 3 green onions, chopped
1^1/2 cups sliced mushrooms
1 to 2 teaspoons soy sauce, or
   to taste
^{1}/2 teaspoon salt
^{1}/2 teaspoon freshly ground
   black pepper

Place the chicken stock, chicken, and ginger in a soup pot. Bring to a boil, reduce the heat, and simmer for 20 minutes. Add the tomatoes, carrot, celery, green onions, mushrooms, soy sauce, salt, and pepper. Simmer for 5 minutes. Drain the noodles and add to the chicken mixture. Cover and cook an additional 5 minutes, or until the noodles are translucent. Serve in bowls.

NOTE: Impale the tomato on the tines of a fork and immerse it in boiling water for 10 seconds. The skin will peel off easily.

Michelle Bernstein, host of the Food Network's Melting Pot, *has her mojo working here with these stuffed game hens. This mojo has nothing to do with Austin Powers, but is, in fact, a Cuban, garlic-citrus sauce that is often used as a marinade. It is similar to vinaigrette, but is cooked. Used as a sauce, it is a fantastic accent to grilled meats and seafood. Michelle is a Miami native and chef of Azul restaurant, in the Mandarin Oriental Hotel, where she celebrates the Latin flavors of her hometown blended with Caribbean, French, and Asian influences. Sour, or bitter, oranges, such as Seville, are used in cooked preparations. Their peel is candied and their essential oils are used to flavor liqueur.*

Mojo Marinated Game Hens with Apple Stuffing

Serves 4

4 Cornish hens
2 cups olive oil
12 garlic cloves, finely chopped
1 teaspoon salt
$^1/_2$ teaspoon freshly ground black pepper
Juice of 4 sour oranges (see note)
1 teaspoon ground cumin
$^1/_3$ cup finely chopped cilantro
$^1/_4$ cup finely chopped fresh oregano
Apple Stuffing (recipe follows)

Clean the hens thoroughly, removing the innards but reserving the livers for the stuffing.

To prepare the mojo, heat the olive oil in a saucepan over medium heat. Add the garlic and stir until the garlic turns golden brown. Immediately add the salt, pepper, sour orange juice, cumin, cilantro, and oregano. Remove from the heat and set aside to cool.

Place the Cornish hens in a large covered dish or large plastic bag and pour in the mojo. Refrigerate overnight, or up to 48 hours in advance. Make sure the hens don't sit one on top of another in the bag. Turn the Cornish hens over at least once during the marinating process.

Preheat the oven to 350°F.

Remove the Cornish hens from the bag. Fill each hen with a quarter of the Apple Stuffing. Place the hens on a rack in a roasting pan and roast for about 45 minutes, or until they are golden and their juices run clear when pricked. Baste 4 to 5 times during cooking with leftover marinade. *(continued)*

Apple Stuffing

2 tablespoons olive oil
6 ounces chicken sausage
1 onion, finely diced
3 garlic cloves, crushed
4 Cornish hen livers, chopped
2 Granny Smith apples, peeled and diced
1 tablespoon chopped fresh thyme
1 tablespoon chopped fresh marjoram
2 tablespoons cognac
$\frac{1}{4}$ cup Chicken Stock (page 35)
1 cup crushed matzo

Heat the olive oil in a large sauté pan over medium heat. Cook the sausage for 5 minutes, then remove from the pan with a slotted spoon, but do not discard the oil. Add the onion to the oil in the pan and cook until soft and translucent, about 3 minutes. Add the garlic, livers, apples, herbs, and cognac. Sauté for 5 minutes. Add the chicken stock, and reduce by half, 3 to 5 minutes.

Add the matzo to the mixture. Crumble the sausage, stir it in, and cook for 10 minutes. Allow stuffing to cool long enough to handle.

Once regarded as a strictly gourmet item, duck is entering the mainstream of American cookery and can be found at most major supermarkets. Duck is fattier and richer than chicken. The fat puts some people off, but this recipe cooks out most of the fat, resulting in a nice crispy skin.

At his restaurant Wildwood, in Portland, Oregon, chef Cory Schreiber pairs his duck with an easy, highly flavored Mushroom Spaetzle. In addition to the spaetzle, Cory serves his duck with Red Wine–Braised Cabbage (page 206).

Maple-Glazed Duck Breast with Mushroom Spaetzle

Serves 4

Mushroom Spaetzle (recipe follows)
$2/3$ cup real maple syrup
1 teaspoon chopped fresh thyme
Zest of 1 orange
Vegetable oil
4 boneless duck breasts, skin on, trimmed of excess fat
1 teaspoon salt
1 teaspoon freshly ground black pepper

Prepare the spaetzle up until the point it is to be sautéed in butter.

To prepare the maple glaze, combine the maple syrup, thyme, and orange zest in a small sauté pan and bring to a simmer. Remove from heat and let stand.

Lightly oil the bottoms of two heavy sauté pans or skillets and place over high heat. Season the duck breasts with the salt and pepper and add to the pans, skin-side down. Cook for 4 to 5 minutes, using the fat rendered in cooking to baste the meat. Reduce heat and cook the duck for 10 to 12 minutes, or until the skin is crisp. Turn the breasts over and cook for 1 minute. Baste the duck with a little of the maple glaze. Remove the duck from the heat, cover, and let stand for 5 minutes while you finish the spaetzle.

Mushroom Spaetzle

Serves 4
$1/2$ cup milk
2 tablespoons ground dried
    mushrooms (see note)
1 cup all-purpose flour
1 large egg, beaten
2 tablespoons minced fresh
    herbs, such as thyme, flat-
    leaf parsley, and chives
1 teaspoon salt
$1/2$ teaspoon freshly ground
    white pepper
Vegetable oil spray
1 tablespoon olive oil
2 tablespoons unsalted butter

In a small saucepan, heat the milk over low heat just until it simmers. Remove from the heat, stir in the ground mushrooms, and let stand for 15 minutes. In a large bowl, combine the milk mixture, flour, egg, herbs, salt, and pepper, mixing until smooth. Cover and refrigerate for 1 hour.

Bring a large pot of water to a rolling boil. Coat the inside of a colander or perforated steaming insert with vegetable spray and place over, but not touching, the boiling water. Using a rubber spatula or your hand, quickly press the batter through the holes, about 2 tablespoons at a time. Once all the batter has been forced through the holes, remove the colander or insert. Gently stir the spaetzle and cook for 1 minute. Drain well and toss with the olive oil; set aside until the duck is nearly finished.

To finish the spaetzle, melt the butter over medium-high heat in a 10-inch nonstick skillet. Add the spaetzle, season to taste with salt and pepper, and cook until brown and crispy.

Divide spaetzle among four plates and place a duck breast on top. Drizzle with a little more maple glaze.

NOTE: Use a spice mill or mini-chopper to grind the mushrooms.

PORTLAND, OREGON

Most people know that Portland, Oregon is "green"—that is, environmentally friendly, carefully designed, and run to help people, plants, and animals live in harmony with nature and with one another. But did you know it's really, really *green*? This city of more than 500,000 people, set on the banks of the Willamette River, is positively teeming with gardens, parks, and nature centers—37,000 acres of open space.

There are three public rose gardens, including the International Rose Test Garden in Washington Park, where new varieties of roses are put through their paces. Every summer there's a Rose Festival, with displays, and a parade. Washington Park is also home to the Hoyt Arboretum, with twelve miles of nature trails and 8,000 specimens. Nearby is the Japanese Garden, with five-and-a-half acres, including an authentic tea house. There's also a city-block-size Classical Chinese Garden, called "The Garden of the Awakening Orchid," with an 8,000-

square-foot-pond. The largest municipal park is Forest Park, at 5,000 acres, and the smallest is Mills End Park, at barely twenty-four inches square. (It's a former pothole, planted by a newspaper columnist as a complaint and cheerfully adopted by the city.) Then there's The Grotto, an internationally known Catholic sanctuary set on sixty-two acres of botanical gardens. And that's not to mention the World Forest Institute, which provides information for governments and industry on forest practices and products, and runs the Forest Discovery Center, with exhibits and educational programs. It's no wonder Portlanders are so interested in food—with all that greenery, they must think they live on a really well-appointed farm.

The Chinese were the first significant immigrant population to the Hawaiian Islands in the late 1780s. This is a simple version of glazed roast duck, somewhat similar to Peking duck, but much easier to prepare. Serve it with white rice and pea pods lightly sautéed in butter.

Honolulu Chinese-Style Roast Duck

Serves 4

One 4- to 5-pound duck
$2^1/2$ teaspoons salt
2 stalks green onion, cut into
    2-inch pieces
2 tablespoons chopped
    parsley
1 tablespoon Chinese five-
    spice powder
5 tablespoons soy sauce
1 tablespoon pineapple juice
$1^1/2$ tablespoons sugar
2 garlic cloves, minced
1 tablespoon hoisin sauce

Rinse the duck inside and out and pat dry. Using a metal skewer or other sharp instrument, pierce the bottom and sides (not the breast) of the duck at half-inch intervals. Salt the cavity of the duck and tuck in the green onions and parsley.

In a small bowl, mix together the Chinese five-spice powder, soy sauce, pineapple juice, sugar, garlic, and hoisin. Rub the sauce all over the duck. Reserve any remaining sauce.

Place the duck on the rack of a roasting pan and put it, uncovered, in the refrigerator for 1 hour to dry somewhat.

Preheat the oven to 350°F.

Rub the duck with the sauce again. Roast for $1^1/2$ to 2 hours, depending on the size of the duck. Test for doneness by pricking it with the tip of a sharp knife; the duck is done when its juices run clear.

Matt Rimel is an energetic, passionate, consummate entrepreneur, who is also the quintessential southern California surfer. Not only is he a restaurateur—he has three wildly popular spots in La Jolla—he also runs a small fishing empire that supplies local chefs. The seafood and sushi at Zenbu are among the best I have ever encountered. So I was astonished when I tried this beef dish and found it to be equally phenomenal. The recipe was developed by chef David Traylor, who is obviously at home at sea and on land.

Zenbu Wasabi-Seared Tenderloin

Serves 2

$1/4$ cup wasabi paste (see note)

1 tablespoon mirin (see note)

Four 3-ounce pieces of beef tenderloin, about $1^1/2$ inches thick

Vegetable oil

Wasabi Oil (recipe follows)

Soy Syrup (recipe follows)

Mix together the wasabi paste and the mirin. Two to three hours before cooking, coat each piece of tenderloin with the mixture. Place in refrigerator. When ready to cook, brush the bottom of a cast-iron skillet or other heavy-bottomed skillet with oil. Sear the tenderloin pieces over medium-high heat for about 2 minutes on each side (for medium rare). Place two tenderloin pieces on each plate and drizzle with Wasabi Oil and Soy Syrup.

NOTE: Wasabi, also called Japanese horseradish, is hot and pungent. It's sold in Asian markets and some supermarkets in paste or powder form. Mirin is Japanese rice wine. If your supermarket doesn't carry it, try an Asian market.

Wasabi Oil

$1/2$ cup wasabi paste
$1/4$ cup mirin
$1/2$ cup rice wine vinegar
$1/4$ teaspoon kosher salt
$3/4$ cup canola oil

Combine the wasabi paste, mirin, $1/2$ cup water, rice wine vinegar, and salt in a blender. With the blender running, slowly pour in the oil until the mixture is emulsified. If you have clean squeeze bottles, put the mixture into one. Otherwise, you can put it in a small bowl and use a spoon to drizzle it.

Soy Syrup

4 cups Chicken Stock (page 35)
1 cup soy sauce
$1/2$ cup mirin
$1/2$ cup dashi-no-moto (see note)

Place all ingredients in a saucepan over medium heat and reduce to the consistency of syrup, 15 to 20 minutes. Let cool and pour into squeeze bottle or small bowl.

NOTE: Dashi-no-moto is a Japanese fish stock. It's available at Asian markets.

This hearty and satisfying one-pot meal gives one the ballast necessary to survive a frigid northern winter. One of the things that makes it so good is that it uses corned beef brisket, not known for being a particularly lean meat, but the virtues of the variety of good root vegetables easily outweigh the small sin of a little fat. Some people like to serve this dish on St. Patrick's Day, but it's good enough to serve all year. Traditionally, it is served with boiled beets.

New England Boiled Dinner

Serves 6 to 8

1 corned beef brisket, about 4 to 5 pounds
24 black peppercorns
1 teaspoon pickling spices
2 bay leaves
6 medium potatoes, peeled and quartered
6 carrots, quartered
3 small turnips, peeled and quartered
4 small parsnips, peeled and halved
12 pearl onions, peeled
1 medium head green cabbage, cut into large wedges and cored
Horseradish-Mustard Cream (recipe follows)

Rinse the brisket under cold running water to wash off the surface brine. Place the brisket in a large pot, such as a stock pot, with enough water to cover.

Cut a 6-inch square of cheesecloth and in the center place the peppercorns, pickling spices, and bay leaves. Pull the sides up to form a bag and tie tightly with kitchen twine. Add to the pot with the brisket. (If they're not confined, the peppercorns have a bad habit of hiding out in the cabbage to surprise unwary diners.)

Bring the pot to a boil. Reduce heat to simmer and cook, skimming as necessary, or until the brisket is tender enough for a fork to penetrate easily, 2 to 3 hours.

Remove the brisket from the pot, cover with foil, and keep warm. (For a leaner dish, remove the brisket and wrap well; refrigerate. Refrigerate the cooking liquid for several hours or overnight. Skim off the congealed fat before proceeding.) Place the potatoes, carrots, turnips, and parsnips in the cooking liquid, and simmer for 15 to 20 minutes, until the vegetables are just becoming tender. Add the pearl onions and simmer for 15 minutes. If desired, skim fat.

Add the cabbage and cook until it is tender, 15 to 20 minutes. Place the brisket on a large platter and slice thinly. Surround with vegetables and sauce. Discard the bag of spices. Serve with Horseradish-Mustard Cream.

Horseradish-Mustard Cream

1 cup sour cream
2 tablespoons grated fresh
  horseradish or bottled, or
  to taste
2 tablespoons coarse-grained
  mustard

Mix all the ingredients together in a small bowl.

This disarmingly simple dish is amazingly good. It's great with oxtails, but it also works perfectly with lamb shanks. In Hawaii, the stew is served with rice, but you can also serve it with potatoes or noodles.

Maui Ranch Oxtail Stew

The recipe comes from a Hawaiian native, Betty Pettus, who grew up on the Big Island of Hawaii, and enjoyed this stew on her visits to a cattle ranch on Maui. Her husband's daughter, Ruth Pettus, and I tested the recipe together, because I just could not believe that with so few ingredients, and virtually no seasonings, this recipe could taste good. It was more than good. This recipe should be part of your regular repertoire.

Serves 6

12 oxtail pieces, or 6 lamb shanks
Four 6-ounce cans tomato paste
6½ cups (about 1½ bottles) dry red wine, such as Cabernet or Merlot
12 garlic cloves, peeled

Place the pieces of oxtail or lamb shanks in the bottom of a heavy pot or Dutch oven. Mix the tomato paste with the red wine in a bowl. Smash 6 of the garlic cloves with the blade of a large knife and add them to the tomato-wine mixture. Pour the mixture into the pot and scatter in the remaining 6 whole cloves of garlic. Bring to a boil, cover, and reduce heat to a low simmer. Cook for 3 to 4 hours, until the meat is tender enough to fall off the bone.

Pork, peaches, and bourbon. We must be in the South—coastal Georgia, to be exact. My friend Tante Anna, of Savannah, is a wonderful cook who delights friends with her locally famous pork specialties such as barbecued spareribs and pulled pork. This slightly braised, hooch-infused platter of chops, sweetened with fresh peaches, is simply divine.

Pork Chops with Caramelized Peaches and Bourbon

Serves 4

4 loin pork chops, about 1 inch thick
Marinade (recipe follows)
$^1/_4$ cup vegetable oil
$^1/_2$ teaspoon salt
$^1/_4$ teaspoon freshly ground black pepper
4 tablespoons ($^1/_2$ stick) butter
1 onion, finely diced
2 garlic cloves, minced
$^1/_4$ cup bourbon
$^3/_4$ cup canned beef broth
3 tablespoons firmly packed dark brown sugar
3 tablespoons cider vinegar
$^1/_2$ teaspoon ground cinnamon
$^1/_4$ teaspoon ground cloves
2 cups peaches (3 to 5 peaches), blanched, peeled, pitted, and sliced (see note)

Place the pork chops in a single layer in a glass baking dish and pour marinade over. Cover and refrigerate for 1 hour. Turn once or twice during marinating process.

Heat the oil in a large skillet or Dutch oven. Remove the pork chops from the marinade, dry off with paper towels, and sprinkle with the salt and pepper. Over medium-high heat, quickly sear the pork chops on both sides until browned, about 3 minutes per side. Remove the pork chops to a plate or pan and keep warm.

Melt the butter in the skillet and sauté the onion and garlic until the onion is translucent. Increase the heat to high and pour in the bourbon. Bring to a boil. Reduce the heat to medium and add the beef broth, brown sugar, cider vinegar, cinnamon, cloves, and peaches and cook, stirring occasionally, for 10 minutes.

Return the pork chops to the pan, coat with some of the sauce, cover, and simmer for 15 minutes. To serve, place the pork chops on plates and spoon peaches and sauce over them.

NOTE: To blanch peaches, immerse them in a pot of boiling water for 30 seconds. Pull off the peel with a paring knife.

Marinade

1/2 cup red-wine vinegar
1/2 medium onion, grated
4 garlic cloves, minced
1/2 teaspoon ground sage
1/4 teaspoon ground nutmeg
1/2 teaspoon freshly ground
    black pepper
3/4 cup olive oil

Mix the vinegar, onion, garlic, sage, nutmeg, and pepper in a small bowl. Whisk in the olive oil, a little at a time, until it is all incorporated.

I have family in Oregon and love visiting Portland. It is an area of our country blessed with an abundance of high-quality produce, fruits, berries, and magnificent seafood and game. On my last visit, I stopped at Higgins, the namesake restaurant of well-known Portland chef and restaurateur Greg Higgins. A member of the Chefs Collaborative, Greg is dedicated to using the best of the locally grown and locally produced products. He not only buys locally, but also has established his own sizable garden and grows vegetables for the restaurant.

The Pacific Northwest is well known for lamb, and here Greg presents a classic preparation, rounding off the feast with his "white puree" of potatoes and root vegetables, Pacific Northwest Puree Blanc (page 214), and Willamette Valley Sautéed Greens (page 202).

Herb-Roasted Rack of Oregon Lamb

Serves 4

2 sides lamb racks, Frenched, split into halves (see note)
Salt and freshly ground black pepper
4 tablespoons canola oil
2 cups breadcrumbs
$1/2$ cup mixed chopped fresh herbs, such as rosemary, thyme, parsley, marjoram
$1/4$ cup minced garlic
$1/4$ cup extra virgin olive oil
$1/2$ cup Dijon mustard

Preheat the oven to 400°F.

Season the four pieces of lamb rack with salt and pepper to taste. Sear them on all sides in the canola oil in a hot skillet. Transfer to a roasting pan, bone side down. Mix together the breadcrumbs, herbs, garlic, and olive oil. Spread the mustard over the top of the racks and then top with the herbed bread mixture. Roast in the oven for 20 to 25 minutes, or until an instant-read thermometer reads 130° to 135°F. The crust should be golden brown. Remove from the oven and allow to rest in the pan for 5 to 10 minutes before serving.

NOTE: "Frenching" means removing the meat from the tops of the bones. It makes for an elegant presentation, but it's not absolutely necessary. Have your butcher French the lamb for you.

Vegetable chapters always seem to appear at the back of cookbooks, which is odd considering they are the foundation of most dining experiences. Vegetables star in salads, as side dishes, even as whole meals, and not just for folks who never eat meat. Platters of marinated springtime asparagus; grilled, freshly harvested leeks and corn; lightly dressed baby lettuces with red and yellow pear tomatoes; a robust salad of Bibb lettuce and radicchio with Gorgonzola and toasted hazelnuts—any of these dishes would be a fine beginning to a meal, or even a light meal themselves, with some good bread and a little dessert. In our house, we often made a entire meal from

6 SALADS, VEGETABLES, AND SIDES

serving bowls of creamy mashed potatoes, country green beans, slow-simmered kale or collard greens, homemade applesauce, sliced tomatoes, and corn on the cob.

Today, thanks to global marketing, most vegetables are available all year, but the best produce is strictly seasonal in your locale. When choosing recipes, pick those that feature ingredients in season. Crab, Corn, and Red Pepper Salad says midsummer, when the crabs are freshly caught, when the sweet corn comes in, and when the peppers are as ripe as can be. The American food revolution that began in the 1970s taught everybody that raw or lightly steamed farm-fresh vegetables can become high points of a meal, but luckily that hasn't stopped creative cooks from dressing vegetables up for town—pairing apple with fennel in a crunchy slaw, or leeks with celery and capers in a saffron infusion. Vegetables shine in supporting roles, too—onions, garlic, and bell peppers with black beans or red beans with rice. Take your pick; each recipe here will complement other dishes in the book, or stand alone as a meal in itself.

This recipe makes a refreshing summer salad from some of Maryland's most famous foods, crab and sweet corn. Serve on a bed of butter lettuce, or in a bowl with fresh tortilla chips as a marvelous dip. Although this recipe hails from the Mid-Atlantic region, it works quite well with Dungeness crab also.

Crab, Corn, and Red Pepper Salad

Combine the oil, vinegar, garlic, lime juice, and onion and whisk thoroughly. Add the crab, red pepper, corn, and cilantro. Season with seafood seasoning and salt and pepper to taste and toss well. Cover and chill for 2 hours. Before serving, bring salad back to room temperature. Adjust the seasonings and serve.

Serves 6

3 tablespoons extra virgin olive oil

1 tablespoon sherry vinegar

1 large garlic clove, peeled and mashed

Juice of 1 lime

1 small red onion, finely minced

$1/2$ pound backfin crabmeat, picked over for shells

1 large red bell pepper, cored, seeded, cut in fine dice

6 ears fresh Silver Queen (or other sweet) corn, blanched and cooled, kernels removed

3 tablespoons fresh cilantro leaves

$1/8$ to $1/4$ teaspoon seafood seasoning

Salt and freshly ground black pepper

This recipe, which I developed while traveling in the Santa Barbara area of southern California, demonstrates that fresh fruit, used in unexpected ways, can give a real spark to an ordinary shrimp salad. Here, succulent little apricots spice up a sweet and savory shrimp salad.

South Coast Shrimp Salad

Serves 4

1 pound shrimp
1 teaspoon salt
1/4 cup finely diced red onion
3 tablespoons finely diced
   celery
1 tablespoon finely snipped
   chives
Apricot-Aioli Dressing (recipe
   follows)
2 ripe but firm apricots,
   peeled and pitted
5 cups mesclun salad mix or
   4 cups watercress

Place the shrimp in a large saucepan with enough water to cover. Add the salt and bring to a boil over high heat. Reduce the heat to medium-low and cook just until the shrimp become bright pink all over, 3 to 5 minutes. Don't overcook. Peel and devein the shrimp and cut them into bite-sized pieces.

Place the shrimp, red onion, celery, and chives in a large bowl and stir gently to mix. Add the Apricot-Aioli Dressing and stir to coat. Finely dice one of the apricots and fold it into the salad mixture.

Divide the mesclun mix or watercress evenly among 4 salad plates. Top with equal portions of shrimp salad. Thinly slice the remaining apricot and use to garnish the plates.

Apricot-Aioli Dressing

1/2 cup Major Grey chutney
1/2 cup mayonnaise
2 garlic cloves, minced
1/2 cup sour cream
1 apricot, peeled, pitted, and
   diced

Combine the chutney, mayonnaise, garlic, and sour cream in a small bowl. Fold in the diced apricot.

This fishing village northeast of Boston and America's oldest seaport, is an idyllic place to enjoy a recently harvested lobster. For generations, the ubiquitous lobster has been plentiful in New England, and, after guests dining on a lobster dinner had their fill, any leftovers were transformed into salad. The original recipes always called for a homemade mayonnaise. The classic salad may be prepared using already picked lobster meat sold in a can, but for the true experience, it is best to take a little effort with a freshly cooked lobster.

Gloucester Lobster Salad

Serves 4

1 pound (about 2 cups of pieces) lobster, cooked and chilled

$1/2$ cup finely chopped celery

1 teaspoon chopped fresh tarragon leaves

$3/4$ cup Tangy Tarragon Mayonnaise (recipe follows)

8 butter lettuce leaves, rinsed

Break or cut the lobster meat into bite-sized pieces and place in a bowl. Stir in the celery and tarragon. Add the Tangy Tarragon Mayonnaise and stir well to coat.

Cover the bowl and place in the refrigerator to chill. About 15 minutes to half an hour before serving, place salad plates in the refrigerator to chill as well.

To serve, place 2 butter lettuce leaves on each chilled plate and gently spoon on one-quarter of the lobster mixture. Serve immediately.

Tangy Tarragon Mayonnaise

1 egg yolk, or $1/3$ cup pasteurized liquid eggs

2 tablespoons tarragon vinegar

$1/2$ teaspoon salt

$1/2$ teaspoon dry mustard

1 cup extra virgin olive oil

1 teaspoon finely chopped fresh tarragon

In a bowl large enough to allow for vigorous motion, whisk together the egg, vinegar, salt, and dry mustard until light and well blended. Whisk in some of the oil, drop by drop, until the mixture begins to thicken. Whisking constantly, continue adding the oil in a slow, steady stream, until it is all incorporated. (If the mixture seems to be separating at any point, stop adding oil and whisk vigorously until emulsion is restored.) Fold in the chopped tarragon.

Doris Hicks, seafood technology specialist for the University of Delaware's marine center in Lewes, Delaware, is affectionately known as "Miss Calamari." Besides heading up a marine research center, Doris is the organizer of Delaware's Coast Day Festival, held every fall in Lewes. It features their annual Crab Cake Cook-Off, along with lectures, research displays, ship tours, children's activities, a nautical crafts show, and seafood cooking demonstrations. Doris devised this festive recipe, which pairs poached, mild-flavored squid with fresh fruit. It would make a nice lunch dish accompanied by some crusty bread or served in a big bowl on a summer buffet table. To save time and effort, purchase your squid already cleaned.

Miss Calamari's Squid Fruit Salad

Serves 6

2 tablespoons sugar

1 teaspoon cinnamon

2 pounds squid, cleaned and skinned

4 tablespoons vanilla yogurt

1 large orange, peeled and sectioned

1 cup fresh pineapple chunks

3 tablespoons golden raisins, plumped (see note)

3 tablespoons flaked coconut, toasted (see note)

In a large saucepan, combine 5 cups water, the sugar, and the cinnamon and heat to boiling. Add the squid and simmer for 5 minutes. Drain the squid and rinse lightly with tap water; allow to cool. Combine the yogurt, orange sections, pineapple chunks, and raisins in a serving bowl. Cut the squid into rings, chop the tentacles coarsely, leaving the fins whole, and add to the fruit mixture. Chill for at least 2 hours. Top with toasted coconut just before serving.

NOTE: To "plump" raisins, simply pour enough boiling water over them to cover and allow to stand for about 10 minutes. Drain the water.

To toast coconut, preheat the oven to 325°F. Spread the coconut on a baking sheet and bake for about 10 minutes, stirring frequently, until lightly browned.

Tucked between the Diablo mountain range and Monterey Bay is the town of Salinas, California. It's a spot built on "green gold"—the lettuces, broccoli, and artichokes that are grown here so plentifully. Salinas is the salad bowl of the nation—and what better place to find an innovative composed plate of delicate Bibb lettuce and slightly bitter radicchio with bits of apple, Gorgonzola, and toasted nuts? A loaf of freshly baked olive bread and a touch of extra virgin olive oil for dipping will transform the salad into a lovely luncheon or light dinner entrée. This salad, which is good enough to eat every day, is from Dennis Donohue, of European Vegetable Specialties, Salinas, California.

Salinas Bibb Salad with Gorgonzola and Toasted Hazelnuts

Serves 4

$1/2$ head radicchio, torn into bite-sized pieces

1 tart apple

1 teaspoon lemon juice

2 heads Bibb lettuce, torn into bite-sized pieces

4 ounces Gorgonzola or other blue cheese, crumbled

$1/2$ cup chopped hazelnuts or walnuts, toasted (see note)

Cider-Dijon Dressing (recipe follows)

Soak the radicchio in cold water for 15 minutes, then drain and pat dry. Core and dice the apple, then sprinkle with the lemon juice. In a large bowl, combine the radicchio and Bibb lettuce, apple, Gorgonzola, and toasted nuts. Pour dressing over salad and toss to coat.

NOTE: Preheat the oven to 400°F. Place chopped nuts on a baking sheet and toast until fragrant, about 5 minutes. Watch the nuts carefully to make sure they don't burn.

Cider-Dijon Dressing

$1/3$ cup vegetable oil

3 tablespoons cider vinegar

$1^{1}/2$ tablespoons honey

1 tablespoon Dijon-style mustard

$1/4$ teaspoon salt

Whisk all ingredients together in a small bowl.

Hearts of palm come from the stem of the cabbage palm, Florida's official state tree. If you haven't tried hearts of palm before, it's an enjoyable culinary experience. They have a delightful mild flavor, similar to an artichoke, with a firm yet smooth texture. Due to their unassertive taste, they lend themselves perfectly to marinating, easily incorporating other flavors. This is a totally Floridian recipe combining hearts of palm with ripe avocados. Hearts of palm are most widely available in cans, but can be purchased fresh in Florida.

Tropical Hearts of Palm Salad

Serves 4

Two 7.8-ounce cans hearts of palm, drained, and halved lengthwise

Avocado Dressing (recipe follows)

1/4 cup finely minced red onion

1 medium or 2 small tomatoes, peeled, seeded, and finely chopped (see note)

5 cups mesclun salad mix

Place the hearts of palm in a medium bowl and pour the dressing over them. Mix thoroughly, cover the bowl, and place in the refrigerator for 1 hour. This salad is best served well chilled, so if you like, place 4 salad plates in the refrigerator when you put in the hearts of palm mixture.

Just before serving, prepare the red onion and tomato. Remove the salad mixture from the refrigerator, and take the hearts of palm out of the dressing. Remove the plates from the refrigerator and divide the mesclun mix evenly among them. Fan out equal portions of hearts of palm on each plate. Drizzle dressing over hearts of palm and top dressing with a sprinkling of tomato and red onion.

NOTE: Impale a tomato on the tines of a fork and submerse it in boiling water for 10 seconds. The peel will slip off easily. Press the seeds out with your fingers under running water.

Avocado Dressing

1 small avocado, peeled and
   pitted
$1/4$ cup fresh lime or lemon
   juice
1 tablespoon red wine
   vinegar
1 garlic clove, minced
1 jalapeño, seeds removed,
   finely diced (see note)
$2/3$ cup olive oil

Mash the avocado with a fork or the back of a spoon. Mix in the lime juice, red wine vinegar, garlic, and jalapeño. Beat in the oil, a little at a time, until it is all incorporated.

NOTE: Wear gloves when handling peppers and do not touch bare skin.

PALM TREES

Temperate coastal areas have one thing in common besides water, beaches, and great food: palm trees. Actually, what they have is palms, because palms aren't trees at all—they belong to a group of flowering plants called monocots, which also includes grasses, lilies, corn, iris, and orchids. Palms come in all sizes—the most stately get as tall as 170 feet!—but they're instantly recognizable by their beautiful, fronded leaves. There are between 2,500 and 3,500 species of palms, but only half a dozen of them are native to the continental United States. Most of them are indeed tropical, because they like lots of water and sunshine and they can't tolerate frost. But in the United States, they grow as far north as the Carolinas on the East Coast and as far north as British Columbia on the West Coast. Apart from their striking beauty, palms are prized for their seeds, such as coconuts and dates, and their "cabbage"—hearts of palm—thus making no small contribution to cuisine, coastal and otherwise.

Big Sur on the California coast is without a doubt one of the most beautiful places on earth. There is a magical quality about the groves of tall redwoods, fog wafting in and out over the majestic cliffs, and the soothing pounding waves of the Pacific. Atop the cliffs of Big Sur, with the Santa Lucia Mountains rising sharply behind, sits Esalen Institute, the birthplace of the holistic, alternative healing and education movement. The Institute hosts thousands of visitors from all around the globe each year and maintains a sustainable kitchen operation with its own lush vegetable gardens.

This beautiful composed salad, originated by Britt Galler, assistant kitchen manager, is typical of the wonders the Esalen kitchen team creates.

Big Sur Fennel and Roasted Beet Salad with Walnuts and Gorgonzola Vinaigrette

Serves 4 to 6

$1/2$ cup walnuts, chopped
1 pound beets, trimmed
$1/4$ cup olive oil
Salt and freshly ground black pepper
1 medium fennel bulb, thinly sliced
1 small head radicchio, torn into bite-sized pieces
$1/2$ pound spinach
1 bunch arugula
Gorgonzola Vinaigrette (recipe follows)

Preheat the oven to 400°F. Spread the walnuts on a cookie sheet and toast until fragrant, 3 to 5 minutes. Watch to make sure the nuts don't burn.

Cook the beets, covered in a steaming basket over boiling water, 20 to 25 minutes, or until just barely done. Cool, peel, and slice into small wedges. Grease a cookie sheet or baking pan. Toss the beets with the olive oil and salt and pepper to taste. Spread the beets in a single layer in the greased pan. Roast for 25 minutes and allow to cool. Combine the beets, fennel, radicchio, spinach, arugula, and walnuts in a salad bowl. Toss with Gorgonzola Vinaigrette and serve.

Gorgonzola Vinaigrette

1 shallot, minced
2 tablespoons white wine
  vinegar
1 tablespoon lemon juice
1 teaspoon Dijon mustard
2 ounces Gorgonzola,
  crumbled
$1/4$ cup olive oil
Salt and freshly ground black
  pepper

In a small bowl, whisk the shallot, vinegar, lemon juice, mustard, and Gorgonzola together with a fork. Continuing to whisk, slowly drizzle in the olive oil. Season to taste with salt and pepper.

This recipe was developed at my restaurant, Gertrude's, at the Baltimore Museum of Art, to accompany Southern-Fried Oysters Remoulade (page 130). There's something about the crispness and tartness of the apple, and the wonderful crisp texture and anise flavor of the fennel, that goes perfectly with the tender, briny oysters. Both dishes are a big hit at the restaurant.

Apple-Fennel Coleslaw

Serves 4 to 6

$1/2$ cup mayonnaise

4 tablespoons red wine vinegar

4 tablespoons honey

2 tablespoons apple cider

1 tablespoon horseradish

1 teaspoon Dijon mustard

$1/4$ cup olive oil

Salt and freshly ground black pepper

1 small cabbage, cored and finely sliced or shredded

1 small bulb fennel, trimmed, and finely sliced or shredded

1 large Granny Smith apple, peeled, cored, and diced

In a medium bowl, mix together the mayonnaise, red wine vinegar, honey, apple cider, horseradish, and mustard. Slowly whisk in the olive oil to form an emulsion. Season to taste with salt and pepper.

In a large bowl, toss together the cabbage, fennel, and apple. Add the dressing and mix thoroughly. Cover and refrigerate for at least an hour before serving, to allow flavors to blend.

Thanks to its unique growing conditions, the Willamette Valley just south of Portland, Oregon, is legendary for its bountiful produce. Savvy local restaurateurs establish close contacts with Valley farmers to insure access to the freshest and best greens and vegetables.

Willamette Valley Sautéed Greens

My sister Lynnie, who lives in Portland, loves putting together kale and chard, calling them "kissing cousins." She likes to make this dish in early spring when the leaves are most tender.

Serves 4

4 tablespoons olive oil

2 tablespoons minced shallots

1 tablespoon minced garlic

1 bunch kale, washed, stemmed, and coarsely chopped

1 bunch Swiss chard, washed, stemmed, and coarsely chopped

2 tablespoons aged sherry vinegar

Salt and freshly ground black pepper

Heat the olive oil on medium heat in a sauté pan large enough to accommodate the greens.

Add the shallots and garlic and sauté for 2 to 3 minutes, stirring often and taking care not to brown the garlic. Add the chopped greens and cook, stirring often, for another 4 to 5 minutes, or until the greens are wilted. Add $^1\!/_4$ cup of water and continue cooking for 2 minutes longer. Add the vinegar and season to taste with salt and pepper. Serve immediately.

WILLAMETTE VALLEY, OREGON

Everybody knows about the famous, or infamous, covered bridges of Madison County, Iowa, thanks to the bestselling book and the Clint Eastwood movie based on it. But probably fewer people know about the covered bridges of the Willamette Valley, concentrated in Albany, Cottage Grove, Linn, and Lowell counties in northwest Oregon. There are more than fifty of them scattered between the Cascade Mountains and the coast, built about a hundred years ago as settlers pushed into the state. They covered the bridges to help protect them from the weather and make them last longer. The rain—and the sun—are what make this part of Oregon an agricultural treasure trove where nuts and berries, fruits and vegetables, flowers and Christmas trees thrive. It's home to more than two dozen wineries, most noted for their production of Pinot Noir, Pinot Gris, and Riesling. More of a beer drinker? The valley also produces hops.

Creole is the name given to Louisiana settlers of European, mostly French, origins, who brought their food traditions with them and adapted them to the ingredients available in their new home. Besides retaining a liking for cream and butter, they often started dishes with a traditional trio of ingredients: green pepper, onion, and celery. Stewed tomatoes are a simple dish, and this version keeps the general outlines of the old-fashioned recipe, but adds a little Creole accent.

Creole-Style Stewed Tomatoes

Serves 6

1 tablespoon butter
2 tablespoons finely chopped green pepper
2 tablespoons finely chopped onion
2 tablespoons finely chopped celery
6 cups (about 6 large) tomatoes, peeled, cored, and chopped (see note)
1 teaspoon sugar
Dash Tabasco, optional
Salt and freshly ground black pepper
1 large or 2 small slices French or Italian bread, crust removed and torn into crouton-sized pieces

Melt the butter in a large saucepan over medium heat. Add the green pepper, onion, and celery, and cook for 2 to 3 minutes, or until the onion becomes translucent. Add the tomatoes and the sugar, partially cover, and simmer for about 15 minutes, until the tomatoes are soft, stirring occasionally to prevent sticking or burning. Add the Tabasco, if using, and salt and pepper to taste. Stir. Add the bread pieces and cook until the bread is soft. Adjust seasonings and serve hot or warm.

NOTE: To peel a tomato, impale it on the tines of a fork and immerse in boiling water for 10 seconds. The skin will slip off easily.

CAJUN AND CREOLE CUISINE

What's the difference between Creole and Cajun food? Creole dishes were developed by French or Spanish settlers, often wealthy planters, based on European techniques, with local ingredients. Many were used to the café society of Paris, and re-created it in cosmopolitan New Orleans. The Arcadians—Cajuns—were country folk, and their cuisine was based on simple preparation of available ingredients and includes lots of one-pot dishes. Having said all that, however, it has to be mentioned that many of the ingredients in both styles are the same—lots of rice, lots of seafood and shellfish (crawfish, crabs, oysters, shrimp, and trout), and local beans, vegetables, and pecans. Both often start with a roux, a mix of butter or oil and flour. And both are immensely popular. What's not to like about a coastal spot that's given the world both beignets and blackened redfish, and both gumbo and Bananas Foster?

My grandmother, Gertie, had a way with cabbage, and twice a year, when making her sour beef and dumplings, she would fill the house with the mesmerizing aroma of simmering braised red cabbage. Chef Cory Schreiber, owner of Portland, Oregon's Wildwood Restaurant, prepares an amazing pot of cabbage accented with Merlot and cider to accompany his Maple-Glazed Duck Breast with Mushroom Spaetzle (page 175), which might even be as good as Gertie's.

Red Wine–Braised Cabbage

Serves 4

2 whole cloves
1 teaspoon fennel seeds
1 teaspoon juniper berries
2 tablespoons unsalted butter
1 small red onion, trimmed, halved vertically, and cut into crescents
1 small head red cabbage, cored and thinly sliced
1 teaspoon salt
1 teaspoon freshly ground black pepper
^{1}/2 cup Merlot
^{1}/2 cup apple cider

Grind the cloves, fennel, and juniper in a spice mill or mini-chopper and set aside.

In a 4-quart stock pot, melt the butter over medium heat. Add the onion and sauté for 3 minutes, or until translucent.

Mix in the cabbage, salt, and pepper, and cook until the cabbage begins to wilt. Stir in the wine, cider, and ground spices.

Bring the mixture to a boil. Lower heat, cover, and cook, stirring frequently, for 25 to 30 minutes, or until the cabbage is soft to the bite.

Here is a quick and easy side dish for most fish, poultry, and meat entrées. Chef Christopher Aeby, of Corpus Christi, designed these cumin-scented carrot coins for his signature Corpus Christi Crispy Grouper with Cilantro-Lime Vinaigrette (page 62).

Chris's Cumin Carrots

Serves 4

2 tablespoons butter
3 large carrots, peeled and
　　cut into thin coins
$1/4$ teaspoon ground cumin
Salt and freshly ground black
　　pepper

Bring a pot of lightly salted water to a boil. Put 1 tablespoon of the butter into the boiling water and add the carrot coins. Remove the pot from the heat and allow the carrots to sit in the water for 5 minutes, or until just tender.

Melt the remaining tablespoon of butter in a sauté pan and mix in the cumin.

Drain the carrots and add them to the sauté pan. Heat until warmed through. Season with salt and pepper to taste and serve at once.

It's not just the main dishes that shine at Cory Schreiber's Wildwood restaurant. Always seeking out the freshest local ingredients, Cory treats every element of a meal as an integral note in a symphony of Pacific Northwest flavors.

Saffron-Braised Leeks

He serves these saffron-braised leeks with his Wildwood Planked Salmon, (page 68), but they also go perfectly with any light preparation of fish or chicken. A little secret Cory lets us in on is to save the braising juice and use it as a vinaigrette.

Serves 4

1/2 cup white wine, such as
   Chardonnay
1/2 cup white wine vinegar
1/4 teaspoon saffron threads
1/2 cup olive oil
4 sprigs thyme
12 baby leeks, washed and
   left whole, or 4 regular
   leeks, white part only, cut
   into long, thin strips and
   washed
4 celery stalks, julienned
1 small red onion, thinly
   sliced
2 tablespoons capers, drained
8 cups (about 8 ounces) baby
   greens
1 teaspoon salt
1/2 teaspoon freshly ground
   black pepper
2 large hard-cooked eggs,
   chopped, for garnish

Preheat the oven to 350°F.

In a large skillet, combine the wine, vinegar, and saffron. Heat over medium-low heat for 5 to 6 minutes, or until the saffron "blooms" and the liquid is a bright yellow.

Mix in the oil, thyme, and leeks. Bring to a boil. Remove from the heat and transfer to an ovenproof dish or Dutch oven.

Cover and place in the oven to braise for 8 to 10 minutes. Add the celery, onion, and capers; braise an additional 10 minutes. Let the vegetables cool in the braising liquid. Cover and refrigerate for 2 hours or overnight.

One hour before serving, remove from the refrigerator. Using a slotted spoon, remove the vegetables from the braising liquid, reserving the liquid for another use, and setting the leeks aside. Divide the leeks evenly among 4 plates.

In a large salad bowl, combine the greens and the remaining vegetables with 3 to 4 tablespoons of the braising liquid. Season with the salt and pepper. Toss the salad and place it on top of the leeks. Garnish with the chopped egg.

When settlers first landed on U.S. shores, beans were among the things they brought with them. They were easy to store and transport, they could be cooked in a variety of ways, and they hardly ever met a vegetable or meat they didn't go great with. This bean dish came to be associated with Boston, and it still features ingredients that any self-respecting colonist would have had on hand. The cooking time will vary according to the age of the beans. Older ones will take longer, so you need to keep checking. Serve with boiled franks and Boston Brown Bread (page 228).

Boston-Style Baked Beans

Serves 6 to 8

1 1/2 pounds navy beans, picked over
1 cup molasses
1/4 cup firmly packed brown sugar
1 teaspoon dry mustard
2 teaspoons salt
1/2 teaspoon freshly ground black pepper
1/3 pound salt pork, cut in four pieces
1 teaspoon Worcestershire sauce, optional

Preheat the oven to 300°F.

Place the beans in a large ovenproof pot or Dutch oven and add water to cover. Bring to a boil, skimming foam as necessary. Reduce heat, partially cover, and simmer the beans, stirring occasionally, about 30 minutes, or until they become tender.

Drain the beans, reserving 2 cups of the cooking liquid. Return the reserved cooking liquid to the pot or Dutch oven. Add the molasses, brown sugar, dry mustard, salt, pepper, and 2 pieces of salt pork and bring to a boil. Add the beans and stir to mix thoroughly. Stir in the Worcestershire sauce, if using. Place remaining pieces of salt pork on top.

Cover the pot, place in the oven, and bake for at least 3 and possibly up to 4 hours, until the beans are caramel-colored and thickly syrupy. Watch the beans while they are cooking, and add water if they are becoming too dry. Stir occasionally to make sure beans aren't sticking and to prevent burning. Adjust seasonings and serve.

BOSTON BAKED BEANS ON SATURDAY NIGHT   There is hardly a cookbook that focuses on American cookery that does not include a recipe for Boston Baked Beans. It is a dish that dates back to colonial times and is said to have been slow-baked on Saturdays by the local Puritan women who, because of Sabbath laws, were forbidden to cook on Sunday. They ate the beans first on Saturday evening and would then eat the leftovers on Sunday.

I was speaking with Steve Parkes from Whole Foods' Pigeon Cove seafood operation in Gloucester, Massachusetts, and we were fondly recalling those Saturday night meals in our youth of franks, baked beans, and steamed brown bread. Steve said his mom would prepare the meal ahead so that the clan would have plenty to eat while she and his dad went out on the town for an evening of dancing. Even though my grandmother, Margaret Shields, left Boston well before I was born, I don't believe there was a Saturday night until I moved out on my own that there weren't franks, savory beans, and brown bread on our table. Some traditions just stick.

Cuban cuisine and black beans are virtually synonymous. This basic bean preparation is the foundation of countless Cuban and other Caribbean, Central, and South American meals. This recipe employs the "no-soak" method, meaning the beans are not soaked overnight before cooking. If you prefer to soak your beans (it's said that makes them a little less gassy), simply reduce the cooking time. Watch the beans, as they cook quickly and you do not want them mushy. Chef Tony Piedra, of Miami's Versailles restaurant, says not to forget to serve the beans with white rice.

Cuban-Style Black Beans (*Frijoles Negros a la Cubano*)

Serves 4 to 6

1 pound (about $2^1/2$ cups) black beans, triple-washed and picked over
1 medium onion, finely diced
1 garlic clove, minced
1 green bell pepper, diced
1 bay leaf
1 teaspoon sugar
$^1/2$ teaspoon ground cumin
$^1/2$ teaspoon fresh oregano
4 teaspoons salt
$^1/2$ teaspoon freshly ground black pepper
$^1/2$ cup olive oil

In a stainless steel pot, cook the beans in 6 cups of water over medium heat for about 2 hours, skimming off surface foam frequently. When the beans start getting soft, add the onion, garlic, bell pepper, bay leaf, sugar, cumin, oregano, salt, pepper, and olive oil. Reduce heat to low and simmer until the beans are tender, at least 30 minutes. Stir frequently, and make sure the water level is high enough to keep the beans covered. The beans should be soupy, not dry or swimming in water. Taste and adjust seasoning before serving.

CAFÉ CUBANO   Cuban coffee is similar to espresso—made with dark-roast beans and poured into a small cup in which sugar—a lot of sugar—has already been placed. The coffee itself is usually from South America; it's the sweetness that makes it Cuban. The coffee is sometimes served with a little milk or even liqueur. There's also a Cuban version of *café au lait*, called *café con leche*, made with equal parts of coffee and hot milk. It seems that no matter what side street you turn down in Miami, there are window counters with lines of people of every social stripe, patiently waiting to purchase their daily jolt of the potent brew.

This favorite dish of New Orleans was originally prepared on wash day, which was always on Monday. The humid Gulf air ensured that the wet laundry spent a long time on the line, giving the women a full day to slow-cook the beans. As in other cultures, beans are a staple and a good source of inexpensive protein that may be supplemented with a portion of meat or fish depending on the person's means. I always add the salt near the end of the cooking process, because adding it too early will make the beans tough and they will take longer to cook.

Red Beans and Rice

Serves 6 to 8

1 pound kidney or other
    small red beans, picked
    over
One 8-ounce smoked ham
    hock
1 medium onion, diced
2 celery stalks, trimmed and
    diced
1 medium green pepper,
    diced
2 bay leaves
1 teaspoon dried thyme
1 teaspoon dried oregano
$1/2$ teaspoon cayenne pepper
1 garlic clove, minced
1 large tomato, peeled and
    chopped (see note)
Salt and freshly ground black
    pepper
6 cups cooked rice

Bring $1^{1}/2$ quarts of water to a boil in a large, heavy-bottomed pot. Wash the beans, drain, and add to the pot. Return to a boil and cook for 5 minutes. Remove the pot from the heat and allow the beans to soak in the hot water for 1 hour. Drain the beans again, discard the liquid, and set aside.

Add an additional $1^{1}/2$ quarts of water to the pot, along with the ham hock, onion, celery, green pepper, bay leaves, thyme, oregano, cayenne, and garlic. Bring to a boil and cook for 15 minutes. Add the beans and the tomato. Reduce heat; simmer for 45 minutes, add salt and pepper to taste, and continue simmering for 15 minutes more, or until the beans are tender. Add water if the beans are becoming too dry. If the sauce is too watery near the end of cooking, turn up the heat and reduce quickly. Before serving, remove the ham hock and pick the meat off the bone. Return the meat to the pot. Reheat if necessary. Serve over rice.

NOTE: To peel a tomato, impale it on the tines of a fork and submerse in boiling water for 10 seconds. The skin will pull off easily.

RICE   Rice is grown and eaten nearly all over the world. Nobody knows exactly how old it is; it grows wild in parts of India and Asia, and it's assumed that hunter-gatherers discovered its value possibly as early as 7,000 years ago. Rice was also grown in Africa as far back as 1500 B.C.

Cultivation began in the United States at the time of European settlement. Virginia planters were already experimenting with growing rice—not very successfully—in the late 1600s, when a ship's captain gave a South Carolina planter a bag of rice as a present.

The crop took off there and within years, the state was a major exporter of rice. The success of the rice crop in that Southern state was almost certainly the result of the know-how of West African slaves brought to the cultivation of the labor-intensive crop.

By the early twentieth century, rice was no longer grown as a commercial crop in South Carolina or Georgia. Rice production has moved to other states, mostly coastal—California, Louisiana, Mississippi, and Texas, along with Missouri and Arkansas.

Rice is graded by a ratio of grain length to width: short, long, or medium. Arborio rice, used in risotto, is short-grained, and fragrant jasmine rice is long-grained. Rice is also characterized as waxy or nonwaxy—that is, sticky, as in Japanese sticky rice, or nonsticky. Brown rice is the most healthful form, because it retains more of the natural fiber, but even white rice contains no fat or sodium—that all comes from what you cook and serve it with.

Rice is versatile enough to be breakfast, lunch, dinner, or dessert (who doesn't love rice pudding?), and to be the basis for dishes as down-home as red beans and rice or as elegant as paella.

Chef Greg Higgins of Portland, Oregon, suggests serving this root vegetable trio with his Herb-Roasted Rack of Oregon Lamb (page 187). It is a splendid companion for most roast meats, game, and poultry.

Pacific Northwest Puree Blanc

Serves 4

3 cups peeled and roughly chopped parsnips

3 cups peeled and roughly chopped Yukon Gold potatoes

2 cups peeled and roughly chopped celeriac (celery root)

$1/4$ cup extra virgin olive oil

Salt and freshly ground black pepper

Place the parsnips, potatoes, and celeriac in a saucepan and cover with lightly salted water. Bring to a boil. Cook about 20 minutes, or until tender enough to mash easily. Drain thoroughly and transfer to a mixing bowl. Mash the vegetables to an even texture, add the olive oil and salt and pepper to taste, and mix well. Serve immediately or cover the bowl and keep in a 200°F oven until serving time.

This amazingly simple recipe by Miami chef Michelle Bernstein is a side for her Mojo Marinated Game Hens with Apple Stuffing (page 173). Besides the game hens, the mash works well with almost any Hispanic roasted, grilled, or braised meat or poultry.

Plantains, part of the banana family, are sometimes called a "cooking banana," and for this recipe they must be fully ripe. A really ripe plantain is almost totally black on the outside. Most recipes call for the bananas to be green when it is used as a starch, and not really sweet, as it is here.

Plantain Mash

Serves 4

6 overripe plantains, peeled, cut into 1-inch pieces
1/4 cup spiced rum
1/2 cup dark brown sugar
Juice of 4 limes
Salt and freshly ground black pepper

Combine the plantains, rum, and sugar in a saucepan. Add just enough water to barely cover, and cook until soft, about 10 minutes. Mash with a potato masher or a wooden spoon. Stir in the lime juice and season with salt and pepper to taste.

PLANTAINS, POMEGRANATES, AND NAM PLA   In the past decade or two, a number of economic, political, technological, and social factors have contributed to a major change in the way America shops for food. One thing that happened, back in the 1980s, is that the economy went global. Better preservation, faster shipping, and globalization meant food could be transported all over the world almost as easily (and in some cases more easily) as when it was merely shipped from the country to the city. Suddenly, things that used to be seasonal—like asparagus, citrus fruits, and tomatoes—were available all year round, because when it's winter up here in the Northern Hemisphere, it's summer down there in the southern part of the globe.

Fruits and vegetables from South Africa and Central and South America grace grocery shelves in November and February, where there used to be largely root vegetables and some broccoli from Florida or California. (Since shipping naturally involves ports, coastal areas are big beneficiaries of this trend.)

A little earlier, the end of the Vietnam War, the opening of China to world trade, and the collapse of Communism began to make global travel easier. Ever-changing patterns of immigration brought more new settlers from Mexico and Central America, and from Vietnam, Thailand, and other Pacific Rim countries. Americans were discovering great regional cuisine in the '80s, and chefs were becoming celebrities, getting people to eat things like hot peppers, quinoa, sushi, artichokes, and stir-fried vegetables. Palates lulled to sleep by steak and potatoes woke up to new possibilities.

So the new foods that immigrants brought with them found a receptive audience. Plantains, jicama, chayote, jerk seasoning, chiles hot enough to take the top of your head off; pomegranates and saffron from the Middle East; harissa and raita from India and Mediterranean Africa; fish sauces from Thailand (nam pla) and Vietnam (nuoc nam); and lemongrass, wasabi, and nori (seaweed) from the Far East began to show up on menus and grocery shelves. Ten years ago, groceries that stocked only canned jalapeños and ordinary bananas now have boutique bananas, plantains, and fresh jalapeños in their produce sections. Where there are large ethnic populations, demand may mean everybody can buy jicama and lemongrass. It's a revolution, and a lovely one. These food trends always start on the coasts—usually in California, Florida, or New York—and work their way inland, so eventually, everybody can enjoy a wide, wide world of food.

Outdoor parties beg for potato salad, especially with barbecued meats and grilled fish. There are countless styles of potato salad, and this unique version is a pleasant change from the deli variety. I discovered this recipe on a trip up the coast of California when I took a slight detour to Salinas.

The firm, mustard-scented potatoes are enhanced with brightly colored radicchio leaves, which are folded in at the end. Radicchio's slightly bitter flavor works perfectly in this potato salad. This recipe is from European Vegetable Specialties.

Central Coast Potato Salad

Serves 4 to 6

1 pound small yellow
  potatoes, cooked until
  tender
1/4 cup thinly sliced sweet
  onion
5 tablespoons red wine
  vinegar
4 tablespoons olive oil
1 1/2 tablespoons coarse-grain
  mustard
Salt and freshly ground black
  pepper
1 head radicchio, cored and
  chopped
1/4 cup chopped parsley

Cut the potatoes in halves or quarters, depending on their size, and place in a large bowl with the onion.

In a small bowl, whisk together the vinegar, the olive oil, and the mustard. Add salt and pepper to taste. Pour mixture over potatoes and onions and toss to coat. Fold in the radicchio.

Fold in the parsley and adjust the seasonings. Serve immediately, or cover and chill up to 6 hours.

When I was growing up, my grandmother always kept a can in the freezer to collect the fat left over from frying the morning bacon. Bacon fat is a perfect medium for sautéing onions and potatoes. At Chris Aeby's Lavender Restaurant in Corpus Christi, they toss thin slices of potato in bacon fat and roast them quickly in a hot oven. They are crispy and almost sinfully delicious.

Bacon-Roasted Potatoes

Serves 4

4 medium potatoes
2 tablespoons bacon fat, melted
2 garlic cloves, finely minced
Salt

Preheat the oven to 400°F.

Peel and slice the potatoes 1/4 inch thick. Place in a mixing bowl and coat with the melted bacon fat. Add the garlic and salt to taste and mix well. Place the potatoes on a baking sheet and roast for about 20 minutes.

Jerry Bair of the Mosquito Café, in Galveston, Texas, pairs this updated rendition of the classic Middle Eastern dish with his grilled grouper. Actually, this side dish is perfect with all types of grilled and sautéed fish and poultry. For a light luncheon, try the couscous with a bit of hummus and warm pita bread—it's heavenly.

Gulf Coast Peach-Pecan Couscous

Serves 6

4 cups Vegetable Stock (page 35) or water

$^1/_4$ cup extra virgin olive oil

One 17$^1/_2$-ounce box precooked couscous

2 teaspoons kosher salt

1 cup pecan pieces, toasted (see note)

1 cup dried peaches, cut into thin strips

$^1/_3$ cup chopped Italian parsley

$^1/_3$ cup chopped fresh mint

1 tablespoon fresh ginger, peeled and grated

$^1/_4$ cup fresh lemon juice

Zest of one orange, finely chopped

Salt and freshly ground black pepper

Bring the vegetable stock or water to a boil in a large saucepan.

In a second large saucepan, heat the olive oil and add the couscous, stirring to coat the grains, and sauté for 2 minutes. Remove from the heat and pour in the boiling stock or water and the salt and stir. Cover and set aside to "steam" for 12 to 15 minutes. Remove the lid and fluff the grains with a fork. Set aside.

When the couscous has cooled to room temperature, place it in a medium-size bowl and mix in the toasted pecan pieces, dried peaches, parsley, mint, ginger, lemon juice, and orange zest. Add salt and pepper to taste. Serve at room temperature.

NOTE: Heat the oven to 350°F. Place the pecans on a baking sheet and toast until fragrant, about 10 minutes. Cool.

Dottie Timberlake, the Chesapeake's grand dame of jazz piano and organ, not only can tickle those ivories, but can also whip up some "divalicious" coastal-country dishes. She learned her cooking techniques from her mom, Victoria, a Potomac River lady, who raised her family outside Washington, D.C. Dottie believes, and rightly so, that no self-respecting country cook would throw a party or celebration without an ample supply of homemade macaroni and cheese.

Dottie's Old Time Mac and Cheese

Serves 8 to 10 generously

16 ounces (1 pound) elbow
  macaroni
2 tablespoons butter
2 tablespoons cornstarch
1 can (15 ounces) evaporated
  milk
1 pound sharp cheddar
  cheese, coarsely grated
6 large egg yolks
Coarsely ground black
  pepper
$^1/_2$ cup grated Parmesan
  cheese, or more to taste
Sweet paprika, for garnish
Vegetable oil spray

When you compare this version to anything you can buy packaged or frozen, you'll be glad to spend the little bit of effort to make this first-class, cheese-enriched casserole. Dottie's mom used to dot the top of the casserole with butter "so it would brown up nice," but Dottie uses a light coating of vegetable oil spray to get the same effect.

Cook the macaroni al dente according to package instructions. Drain and rinse well with cold water to stop the cooking process. Drain thoroughly and set aside.

Preheat the oven to 350°F. Lightly grease a 13 x 9-inch glass baking dish.

Melt the butter in a heavy-bottomed saucepan over medium heat. Add the cornstarch and whisk until smooth. Remove from the heat and stir in the evaporated milk. Return to the heat and stir until the mixture begins to thicken. Remove from the heat again and stir in the cheddar cheese. Allow the mixture to cool for 10 minutes, then add the egg yolks and mix well. Add pepper to taste.

Place the macaroni in the prepared baking dish and stir in the cheese mixture. Mix until the pasta is well coated. Sprinkle on the Parmesan cheese and garnish with the paprika. Spray the top of the casserole with vegetable oil or dot with small bits of butter and bake for 30 to 35 minutes, or until the casserole becomes brown around the edges.

When you grow up in the South, you learn to love your grits, but if you're not from there, you may wonder what anyone sees in them. This cheesy casserole, almost like a soufflé, will turn almost everybody into a fan.

Miss Karol's Cheesy-Hot Grits Casserole

I got hooked at a New Year's Day party when my friend Karol Menzie sashayed in with two big containers of these grits. Some of the other party revelers took a bite and commented, "This is delicious—what is it?" This is a great party dish, because no one can resist it.

You can adjust the heat by using more or less of the peppers, and you can substitute just about any cheese. Serve as part of a lunch or supper buffet, or with ham or fried or roast chicken.

Serves 8 to 10

2 cups regular grits
2 teaspoons salt
1 egg
$^{2}/_{3}$ cup milk
8 tablespoons (1 stick) butter, cut in small pieces (optional)
1 cup Monterey Jack cheese with jalapeño peppers, cut in small cubes
2 cups cheddar cheese, shredded
2 jalapeño peppers, seeded and minced (see note)
$^{1}/_{2}$ teaspoon white pepper

Preheat the oven to 325°F.

Cook the grits in a large saucepan or Dutch oven, with water and the 2 teaspoons salt, according to package directions.

In a 1-cup glass measuring cup, whisk the egg with a fork until white and yolk are blended, then add *just enough* milk to measure $^{2}/_{3}$ cup. Whisk to blend.

Add the milk mixture to the grits, along with the butter, if using, Monterey Jack and Cheddar cheeses, minced jalapeños, and white pepper. Cook on moderate heat, stirring constantly, for about 5 minutes. Taste and adjust seasonings.

Transfer the grits to an oven-proof casserole and bake for 45 to 50 minutes, until the top is lightly browned.

NOTE: When you're mincing the jalapeños, wear gloves. You can substitute a small can of minced jalapeños, drained. Or, if you don't want the grits to be so spicy, omit the jalapeño peppers. The jalapeño cheese will still furnish a bit of heat.

Southern Florida is a little bit of heaven-here-on-earth for exotic-fruit lovers. And the gurus of the movement would be Marc and Kiki Ellenby, owners of the LNB Groves in the farming region of Homestead. Not cut in the typical image of southern farmers, the Ellenbys left the frigid Midwest more than twenty years ago to move to Florida to grow exotic fruit. Their passion for succulent tropical fruit is evident when visiting their home kitchen with its plethora of varieties that to the novice defy identification.

Big Bowl Zesty Tropical Salsa

Serves 10 to 12

3 star fruits
1 mango, diced
6 tomatillos, chopped
1 or 2 large tomatoes, diced
1 red onion, finely chopped
1 small habanero pepper or Scotch bonnet pepper, seeds removed, finely chopped (see note)
1 small green pepper, diced
1 small red pepper, diced
1 small yellow pepper, diced
$1/4$ to $1/2$ cup cilantro, chopped
$1/2$ teaspoon salt
Juice of 1 lemon or lime

Carambola—or, as it is better known, star fruit—can be found in most major food stores in the country, but this is a perfect master recipe for fruit salsas of all kinds. Simply replace the star fruit with papaya, pineapple, or melon—whatever you like—and go to town. The habanero and Scotch bonnet peppers in this dish are exceptionally hot. If one of the great-aunts is coming to visit, you may want to substitute jalapeño or serrano chiles.

Marc and Kiki put out a large bowl of the chilled salsa with blue corn chips and say it is "good enough to eat all by itself." The salsa is also the perfect topping for grilled fish and poultry, and a nice substitution for the Salsa Fresca in Señor Calderon's Ceviche (page 46).

Chop two of the star fruits into small pieces and mix together with the mango, tomatillos, tomatoes, onion, hot pepper, green pepper, red pepper, yellow pepper, cilantro, salt, and lemon or lime juice. Slice the third star fruit for garnish. Serve with chips.

NOTE: Wear gloves when handling hot peppers and do not touch bare skin.

SALSA The word *salsa* means sauce in Spanish and can be attached to any kind of sauce, from applesauce to mayonnaise to tomato sauce to *holandesa*. However, what most people think of when they think *salsa* is a fresh, uncooked, tomato-based, coarse-textured concoction "heated" with chile peppers that is eaten as a snack with chips or crackers. At least, that's what everybody learned in the last decade or so during a meteoric rise in the popularity of Latin-based and "Tex-Mex" food. But salsas don't have to have tomatoes, and in some cases, ingredients may be cooked or grilled. Fruits such as mangoes, peaches, even cherries (see page 225) can serve as the basis for salsa. Onions, garlic, citrus juices, and cilantro are frequent additions. And hold the chips; salsas are great with fish, poultry, and some of the more robust ones add a nice snap to meats and game.

Folks in the Pacific Northwest are proud as punch of their luscious locally grown fruit, cherries being one of the favorites. I think most people think of pies when handed a fresh-picked sack of cherries, but as this recipe shows, it is quite the versatile fruit. The salsa works beautifully with much of the Pacific Northwest seafood: wild salmon, sturgeon, and halibut. But one need not even go to that much effort; a simple bowl of tortilla chips will suffice.

Pacific Punch Cherry Salsa

Serves 6 to 8

3 cups sweet cherries, pitted
$1/4$ cup finely diced red bell pepper
$1/4$ cup finely diced yellow bell pepper
$1/2$ cup finely diced red onion
2 tablespoons honey
2 tablespoons lime juice
1 garlic clove, minced
1 jalapeño or serrano chile, finely diced (see note)
1 teaspoon grated lime zest
Pinch of salt

Chop $2^3/4$ cups of the cherries. Place the remaining $1/4$ cup of cherries in a blender with $1/4$ cup water and puree. In a large bowl, mix the chopped cherries, cherry puree, bell peppers, onion, honey, lime juice, garlic, chile, lime zest, and salt. Cover and let sit for 20 to 30 minutes, to allow the flavors to blend.

NOTE: Wear gloves when handling chiles and do not touch bare skin.

Biscuits and cornbread, muffins, sweet breads, and scones not only make mighty fine eating, they also put smiles on people's faces. These are staples of coastal cuisine, from the brown bread of Boston to the beignets of New Orleans. The world seems to be divided into two groups—those who just love whipping up something to

7 THE COASTAL
BREAD BASKET

bake and popping it in the oven, and those who regard baking as a sort of chemistry test. But baking is really easy. Almost every recipe is the same. You mix the dry ingredients (flour, salt, baking powder) together, you mix the wet ingredients (shortening, eggs) together, and then you combine the two. Add other flavorings (blueberries, zucchini), put in a pan, and put the pan in the oven. Biscuits are even easier: You mix the dry ingredients, cut in the shortening, add just enough liquid to form a ball, knead briefly, roll out, cut out, and bake. Once you're confident with these simple preparations, you can move on to risen bread. Warning: Once you start baking, it may be hard to stop!

This is the traditional accompaniment to Boston-Style Baked Beans (page 209), but it's also good as a tea bread, topped with cream cheese and raisins or cream cheese and slices of pimento-stuffed olives. Steaming the bread is the traditional method of cooking. You can use a pudding mold, but there's something appealing about recycling a coffee tin for this lovely, old-fashioned recipe.

Boston Brown Bread

Makes 1 loaf

2 tablespoons butter
$1/2$ cup rye flour
$1/2$ cup whole wheat flour
$1/2$ cup cornmeal
1 teaspoon baking soda
$1/2$ teaspoon salt
$1/2$ cup molasses or maple syrup
1 cup buttermilk

Grease a pudding mold or 1-pound coffee tin with the butter.

Mix the rye flour, whole-wheat flour, cornmeal, baking soda, and salt in a large bowl. In a separate bowl, thoroughly whisk together the molasses or syrup and the buttermilk. Pour the buttermilk mixture into the flour mixture and stir to incorporate.

Pour the batter into the prepared pudding mold or coffee tin. Cover tightly with foil and place in a deep kettle or stock pot. Add boiling water to a depth of halfway up the mold, cover the kettle, and steam over medium-high heat for 2 hours. If the water level drops, add more water. When the bread is finished steaming, remove it from the kettle and let stand for 15 minutes before unmolding. Run a thin, sharp knife around the inside edge of the mold or can and invert to unmold the bread. Serve warm or at room temperature.

My good friend Linda Gerson is from the deep coastal South, in Alabama. We would regularly eat handfuls of Priester's pecans and cook up batches of this wonderful cornbread in Berkeley, California, to warm our homesick hearts. There is just something about cornbread that brings back so many wonderful memories.

Anyhow, to get back to the story, Linda said that Miss Cook, from down the road, made the absolute best cornbread by getting a cast-iron skillet that had been rubbed with bacon grease extremely hot, and then pouring in the batter and baking until golden brown. This method makes for the best-flavored, crusty cornbread bottom one could imagine. God love Miss Cook.

South of the Mason-Dixon Line Cornbread

Serves 8

1 cup cornmeal
1 cup all-purpose flour
4 teaspoons baking powder
1 tablespoon sugar
1 teaspoon salt
$1/8$ teaspoon white pepper
1 egg, lightly beaten
1 cup milk
4 tablespoons ($1/2$ stick) butter, melted
5 tablespoons bacon or sausage drippings

Preheat the oven to 425°F.

In a large mixing bowl, stir together the cornmeal, flour, baking powder, sugar, salt, and white pepper. Mix together the egg, milk, and melted butter in a separate bowl and add to the dry ingredients. Beat with a wooden spoon until the batter is smooth. Do not overmix.

Pour the bacon drippings into a cast-iron skillet and tilt the pan to distribute evenly. Place the skillet in the hot oven for 5 minutes. Remove the skillet from the oven and pour in the batter. Return it to the oven and bake for 25 to 30 minutes, until the top is golden brown. Remove the cornbread from the oven and let cool in the skillet for a few minutes, then turn the skillet over on a plate, so the bottom of the cornbread cooked in drippings is now the top. Let cool until warm, then slice into wedges and serve with sweet butter on the side.

MASON-DIXON LINE

The Mason-Dixon Line is named for a couple of British astronomers, Charles Mason and Jeremiah Dixon, who between 1763 and 1767 performed a survey for the Calverts, who owned Maryland, and the Penns, who owned Pennsylvania. The survey established the north-south border between the two areas, and the east-west border of Maryland and Delaware. This is the historical Mason-Dixon Line. Long after Mason and Dixon had packed up and gone home to England, the "line" acquired all sorts of other connotations: the boundary between the free North and the slave-owning South, or the boundary between Union and Confederate states in the Civil War. Most people don't even know about the survey of the line separating Maryland and Delaware, and the part people do know about, between Pennsylvania and Maryland, isn't all that long, about 244 miles—just from the north-easternmost point in Maryland to thirty-some miles short of the northwesternmost edge, where Mason and Dixon ran into a little opposition from the Native American inhabitants and decided to retreat. It was enough to settle the dispute between the Penns and the Calverts . . . unless you count the hostility that still persists between the Phillies and the Orioles.

Hush puppies are experiencing a renaissance of sorts these days. A southern specialty not usually found above the Mason-Dixon Line, they are now being gussied up with the likes of fire-roasted corn or caramelized poblano chiles at upscale restaurants all over the country. That's quite the rise in culinary stature from the days when housewives and cooks threw the fried bits of cornbread batter to the dogs to keep them from yapping. I generally still keep mine relatively simple and love them with fried catfish and Leroy's Punta Gorda Shrimp Creole on the side (page 158). Try dusting the puppies with powdered sugar for a real treat.

Old-Fashioned Hush Puppies

Makes about 24

1¼ cups cornmeal
¾ cups all-purpose flour
2 teaspoons baking powder
1 teaspoon salt
1 teaspoon sugar
⅛ teaspoon cayenne pepper
1 tablespoon finely chopped onion
1 tablespoon finely chopped scallion
1 egg, beaten
2 tablespoons vegetable shortening, melted and cooled
¾ cup milk
Vegetable oil, for frying
Powdered sugar, optional

Place the cornmeal, flour, baking powder, salt, sugar, and cayenne in a large bowl and mix together. In a separate bowl, mix together the onion, scallion, egg, shortening, and milk. Using a spoon, beat the wet ingredients into the dry ingredients, a little at a time.

Pour vegetable oil into a skillet to a depth of 1½ inches and heat until very hot, about 375°F. Drop the batter by tablespoonfuls into the oil and fry, a few at a time, until golden brown on all sides. Remove with a slotted spoon and drain on paper towels. Dust with powdered sugar, if desired, and serve hot.

The bountiful gardens of the Esalen Institute, on the gorgeous Big Sur coast in California, produce a bumper crop of zucchini each season. Judging from my summer garden, it seems a similar phenomenon takes place in many coastal gardens. This terrific recipe for the prolific zucchini was developed by Britt Galler, assistant kitchen manager at Esalen.

Esalen Zucchini Poppyseed Bread

Preheat the oven to 350°F.

Makes 1 large
or 2 small loaves

3 cups all-purpose flour
3/4 teaspoon salt
1/2 teaspoon baking powder
1 teaspoon baking soda
1 tablespoon lemon zest
1/4 cup poppy seeds
1/2 pound (2 sticks) butter,
    melted and cooled
2 eggs
2 cups firmly packed brown
    sugar
1 teaspoon vanilla
2 cups shredded zucchini

Grease one 10 x 5-inch loaf pan, or two 8 x 4-inch loaf pans.

Sift together the flour, salt, baking powder, baking soda, lemon zest, and poppy seeds into a bowl. In a separate bowl, whisk together the butter, eggs, brown sugar, and vanilla.

Add the flour mixture to the butter mixture, a cup at a time, beating with a spoon to combine thoroughly. Gently fold in the zucchini. Fill loaf pan or pans and bake until the sides pull away from the pan and a toothpick inserted in the center comes out clean, 60 to 75 minutes.

BIG SUR, CALIFORNIA

Plenty of people who have never been there know exactly what California's Big Sur area looks like: the succession of steep cliffs shearing off into long tails in the choppy waters of the Pacific Ocean below. It's a famous landscape that's been rendered by countless artists. Fortunately, no amount of lithographic overexposure can dim the experience of actually seeing this surreally gorgeous place.

Unlike some spectacular scenery, this is completely accessible, as you can drive the shore-hugging Highway 1 from Carmel to San Simeon, William Randolph Hearst's famed "castle." There's plenty to look at besides the cliffs and the water: Big Sur is the home of the Esalen Institute, an alternative education center that employs meditation, massage, and other sensory-awareness techniques to expand consciousness; exquisite inns, such as Ventana; and the Nepenthe restaurant, on a cliff above the water, a fine place to go for drinks at sunset.

And there is wildlife—in the water, in the trees, and in the air—from blue whales (the world's largest mammal, at up to 100 feet long), to California gray whales, to condors, to elephant seals, to playful sea otters. With so much going on, it's easy to get caught up in an agenda. But it's better to pay attention to the advice of the Big Sur Chamber of Commerce, which urges visitors to stop, relax, and *Do nothing.*

No self-respecting New Englander would take tea without scones, and the residents of the charming village of Wellfleet, Massachusetts, on Cape Cod, are no exception. This version uses Massachusetts's signature berry, the cranberry. You haven't really lived until you've seen a Cape cranberry harvest, when they flood the bogs and beat the bushes so the berries rise to the surface of the water in swirls of every shade of red from pink to burgundy, but mostly in such a clear, pure crimson it takes your breath away.

Wellfleet Cranberry Scones

Makes 10 to 12

2 cups all-purpose flour
2 tablespoons sugar
$^1/_2$ teaspoon salt
3 teaspoon baking powder
4 tablespoons ($^1/_2$ stick) cold
  butter, cut into small
  pieces
2 eggs
$^1/_2$ cup heavy cream
$^1/_4$ cup milk
$^3/_4$ cup dried cranberries

Preheat the oven to 425°F.

Mix together the flour, 1 tablespoon of sugar, the salt, and baking powder in a large mixing bowl. Using a fork or pastry cutter, cut in the cold butter until thoroughly blended.

In a separate bowl, whisk together the eggs, cream, and milk. Working quickly, combine the flour mixture with the egg mixture just until incorporated. Do not overmix. Fold the dried cranberries into the batter.

Turn the dough out onto a lightly floured surface and knead it for 1 minute. It should be a little sticky, but if it is too wet, add just a tiny bit of flour.

Press the dough into a circle about $^3/_4$ inch thick. Sprinkle with the remaining tablespoon of sugar. Cut into 10 to 12 wedges and place them on an ungreased baking sheet. Bake for 15 minutes, or until the scones are golden brown.

CRANBERRIES   Cranberries are one of three fruits native to North America (blueberries and Concord grapes are the other two), and were used at least as far back as the sixteenth century as food, as medicine, and as a dye. Commercial cultivation began in the early nineteenth century at Dennis, Massachusetts, on Cape Cod. The berries do indeed have health benefits—nineteenth-century ships' captains made sure there were cranberries on board for long voyages to prevent scurvy, and recent research indicates that cranberries contain bacteria-blocking compounds that can help prevent ulcers, gum disease, and urinary tract infections. Cranberries grow on trailing vines in gravelly, clayey, peaty, sandy, moist soil, areas known as bogs. Farmers separate bogs with dikes, and when it's time to harvest the berries, they flood the bogs and use special machines to separate the berries from the vines. The berries rise to the top of the water and are gathered in battens and vacuumed up. It's not just efficient; it's probably the most beautiful harvest sight in the world. Most people encounter cranberries in sauce at Thanksgiving, but they can also be used like other berries in baked goods (see Wellfleet Cranberry Scones, page 236).

"Betcha can't eat just one" is a slogan that could easily apply to the delectable, traditional "doughnuts" of the New Orleans French Market. A couple of these heavenly beignets and a good café au lait should get any day off to a great start.

Bourbon Street Beignets

Makes about 5 dozen

1 package active dry yeast
$^1/_3$ cup sugar
$1^1/_2$ teaspoons salt
3 large eggs
1 cup evaporated milk
1 tablespoon grated orange
  zest
7 cups all-purpose flour
2 tablespoons vegetable
  shortening
2 tablespoons butter,
  softened
1 cup toasted pecan pieces
  (see note)
Vegetable oil, for deep-frying
Confectioners' sugar

Unlike conventional doughnuts, significant for their round shape and center holes, beignets are rectangular, like little pillows—a fitting shape for such a comforting snack. I have improvised a bit on the recipe by adding a touch of orange zest and toasted pecans. The only catch is that the dough has to be made a day ahead and refrigerated overnight. However, the dough will keep well in the refrigerator for about a week.

Place $1^1/_2$ cups warm water (105° to 110°F) into a large bowl, then sprinkle in the dry yeast and stir until completely dissolved. Add the sugar, salt, eggs, evaporated milk, and orange zest. Stir in 4 cups of the flour, one cup at a time, and mix with a spoon until smooth. Stir in the shortening and butter. Work in the pecans and then add the remaining flour, about $^1/_2$ cup at a time.

If the dough becomes too stiff to work in the flour with a spoon, pour the mixture onto a lightly floured board and continue working in the remaining flour by hand, kneading gently. Return the dough to the bowl, cover, and refrigerate overnight.

Roll the dough out on a lightly floured board to a thickness of about $^1/_8$ inch. With a sharp knife that has been dipped in flour, cut the dough into 2 x 3-inch rectangles.

Pour oil into a skillet to a depth of 1 inch. Heat the oil over medium heat to 375°F. Fry the beignets in small batches, 3 or 4 at a time, turning them once or twice until they are puffy and golden brown, about 2 to 3 minutes. Remove the beignets with a slotted spoon or tongs to paper towels to drain.

Beignets may be kept warm by placing them in a 200°F oven while you are frying the remaining batches. Sprinkle with confectioner's sugar and serve hot.

NOTE: To toast the pecans, preheat the oven to 400°F. Spread the pecans on a baking sheet and toast until fragrant, about 5 minutes. Watch carefully so the nuts don't burn.

BUÑUELOS, A TASTY TWIST ON TORTILLAS   Rosario Carrizo always looked forward to a certain Christmas tradition. The Corpus Christi, Texas, woman has fond memories of *buñuelos,* the cinnamon sugar–covered fried tortilla chips her family made for the holidays. "We always looked forward to it, every year."

These days, Rosario is the owner of La Malinche Tortilla Factory, which produces most of the flour and corn tortillas and tortilla chips consumed around Corpus Christi. Making *buñuelos* is a simple preparation, as Rosario describes it. You start with an eight-inch flour tortilla. (Tortilla dough is just flour and shortening and a little bit of salt. To moisten the dough, Rosario's family used cinnamon water—water in which a little cinnamon has been boiled.) Mix some cinnamon and sugar together, and set aside. Fry the tortillas in an inch or so of oil. "They puff up—you need to be pressing them down so the oil can go over the top. You want them to be nice and brown—nice and toasty." Let them dry a little on paper towels, then sprinkle over the cinnamon-sugar mix, and "they're good to go." Rosario says *buñuelos* are especially good on a cold winter's day with hot chocolate.

Gravy, grits, country ham, fried chicken . . . There are just some foods that aren't complete without buttermilk biscuits. Biscuits are simple to make and well worth the small effort for that extraordinary homemade taste. They're good just as they are, but for a fancier biscuit, add a tablespoon of very finely chopped fresh rosemary or basil with the buttermilk.

Old-Time Buttermilk Biscuits

Preheat the oven to 350°F.

Makes about 2 dozen
2 cups all-purpose flour
1 tablespoon baking powder
1/4 teaspoon baking soda
1/2 teaspoon salt
6 tablespoons (3/4 stick) cold
    butter, cut in small pieces
3/4 cup buttermilk

Sift together the flour, baking powder, baking soda, and salt into a large mixing bowl. Using a fork or pastry cutter, cut in the butter until the mixture resembles coarse meal. Don't overwork; the less the dough is handled, the flakier the biscuits will be. Add the buttermilk and mix just until the dry ingredients are moistened.

Dust your hands with flour and form the dough into a ball. Turn the dough out onto a lightly floured surface and knead for 1 minute. Roll the dough from the center out to a thickness of about 1/2 inch. Use a 2-inch cookie cutter or biscuit cutter to cut out the biscuits. Place them on a baking sheet and bake for 10 to 12 minutes, or until golden brown.

Blueberry muffins are a perennial favorite, but these may be the best you'll ever eat. On the Pacific Northwest coast, they're particularly proud of their local berries and nuts, but no matter where you live, you can enjoy this great combination of flavors. Toasting the hazelnuts deepens and sweetens the flavor.

Portland Blueberry-Lemon-Hazelnut Muffins

Preheat the oven to 400°F.

Makes 1 dozen

1/2 cup hazelnuts
1/4 cup melted butter, plus
   1 tablespoon
2 cups all-purpose flour
4 teaspoons baking powder
1/2 cup sugar
1/2 teaspoon salt
1 egg, slightly beaten
1 cup milk
1 1/2 teaspoons lemon zest
1 cup blueberries

Coarsely chop the hazelnuts, spread them on a cookie sheet, and toast until fragrant, about 5 minutes. Watch carefully so the nuts don't burn. Set aside.

Lower the oven temperature to 375°F. Use 1 tablespoon of the butter to grease a 12-cup muffin tin.

Mix together the flour, baking powder, sugar, and salt in a large mixing bowl. In a separate bowl, whisk together the 1/4 cup of melted butter, the egg, and the milk until blended. Stir the flour mixture into the butter-egg mixture just until the batter is thoroughly moist. Do not overmix. The batter will be thick and lumpy. Fold in the lemon zest, blueberries, and hazelnuts.

Spoon the batter into the muffin tins, filling each well about two-thirds full. Bake until the muffins are uniformly brown, about 25 to 30 minutes. A toothpick inserted in the center should come out clean. Remove the muffins from the oven and let stand about 5 minutes. Serve warm, or at room temperature.

Desserts are the much-anticipated finish to a memorable meal. I frequently talk with people who love to cook, and I have not found any other type of recipe that inspires the excitement, the enthusiasm, the pride, and the sense of history that desserts do. People love bringing desserts to a potluck dinner, especially when there's just a little competition to come up with something exciting. A lot of traditional dessert recipes get handed down from generation to generation, and some tend to run in families—

8 DESSERTS

there are families that specialize in baking cakes, and others that prefer making pies.

As in our other dishes, regional ingredients define our

desserts: apples in New England; peaches and pecans in the Carolinas, Georgia, and along the Gulf Coast; coconut in Hawaii; berries in the Great Lakes and Pacific Northwest. This collection includes a mix of truly traditional, comfort-food recipes, such as blackberry cobbler and rice pudding, updated a bit for the new century, with a few newer, innovative things—such as a bread pudding made with the Latin dulce de leche, and a cheesecake made with goat cheese. These are family-style dishes, brought to the table whole, usually just-baked, and sliced or scooped onto individual plates. These are the kind of desserts I remember from my childhood, with the family around the table, served with plenty of conversation and banter, a festive and fitting close to a happy occasion.

Fourth-generation Louisiana shrimper Leroy Devine looks forward each year to the arrival of Twelfth Night, January 6, because that's when his wife, Honey, starts making her King Cake, a traditional French dessert that kicks off the Lenten season. There are almost as many versions of King Cake as there are Mardi Gras parties in New Orleans, but all the recipes agree on a few points: The batter is a sweet, yeast coffee-cake type, the dough has cinnamon or nutmeg in it, and the icing is decorated with colored sugar in the Mardi Gras colors of purple for justice, green for faith, and gold for power. And, oh yes, the cake contains a "baby"—either a tiny doll or a bean, or sometimes even a piece of jewelry. The person who gets the piece with the baby may or may not become the king or queen of the party, but he or she is pretty sure to get tagged with being host of the next party. King Cakes are so widely available commercially in New Orleans that hardly anybody bakes their own, but if you live someplace else and want to celebrate carnival time just before the austerities of Lent, the cake is time-consuming, but not hard to make. And it's fun to do the decoration.

Miss Honey's King Cake

Serves 10 to 12

2 packages active dry yeast

$1/2$ cup plus 1 teaspoon sugar

$3^1/2$ to $4^1/2$ cups unsifted all-purpose flour

1 teaspoon nutmeg

2 teaspoons salt

1 teaspoon lemon zest

$1/2$ cup plus 1 tablespoon warm milk

5 egg yolks

10 tablespoons butter, softened

1 egg, lightly beaten

1 teaspoon cinnamon

1 "baby" (doll, bean, or jewelry)

FOR THE GLAZE:

2 tablespoons lemon juice

1 teaspoon vanilla extract

1 cup confectioners' sugar

FOR THE DECORATIONS:

$1^1/2$ cups sugar

2 drops each green, yellow, and purple (red and blue mixed) food coloring

Dissolve the yeast and the teaspoon of sugar in $1/2$ cup lukewarm water (110° to 115°F) and let stand until foamy, about 5 minutes. Combine the remaining sugar, $3^1/2$ cups flour, nutmeg, and salt, and sift together into a large mixing bowl.

In a small bowl, mix the lemon zest and $1/2$ cup milk with the yeast mixture. Make a well in the center of the flour and pour in the yeast-milk mixture. Add the egg yolks. Using a wooden spoon, beat in 8 tablespoons of the butter, 1 tablespoon at a time. Continue to beat for 2 minutes or until the dough can be formed into a medium-soft ball.

Place the dough on a lightly floured board and knead, adding more flour as needed until the dough is no longer sticky. When all the flour is incorporated, continue kneading the dough for about 10 more minutes, or until it is shiny and elastic.

Coat the inside of a large bowl evenly with 1 tablespoon of the softened butter. Place the dough in a bowl, and turn to coat the dough on all sides. Cover with a tea towel and let stand in a warm place to rise until doubled in bulk, about $1^{1}/2$ hours.

Grease a large baking sheet with the final tablespoon of butter and set aside. After the dough has completed its rising, punch it down and turn it out onto the lightly floured board. Roll and shape the dough into a long "snake" or cylinder (about $2^{1}/2$ inches in thickness), and then sprinkle with the cinnamon.

Fold the long cylinder in half end to end and pinch the ends together. Then twist the dough. Turn the twist into a ring and pinch the ends together. (The idea here is to try and form the dough into the shape of a crown.)

Place the formed dough on the buttered baking sheet and cover with a towel, allowing it to rise in a warm place for 45 minutes, or until doubled in volume.

Preheat the oven to 375°F.

After the second rising, mix the beaten egg with the remaining 1 tablespoon of milk and lightly brush the top and sides of the cake with the mixture. Bake for 25 to 35 minutes, or until golden brown. Remove from baking sheet to wire rack to cool. Tuck the "baby" into the cake from underneath.

(continued)

To make the glaze, mix the lemon juice and vanilla in a bowl. Add the confectioners' sugar a little at a time, stirring to make a smooth mixture. When it reaches a thick pouring consistency, drizzle it all over the cake.

TO MAKE THE SUGAR DECORATIONS: Put $\frac{1}{2}$ cup sugar and 1 to 2 drops of green food coloring in a jar. Put the lid on the jar and shake vigorously to mix the colors together evenly. Repeat with another $\frac{1}{2}$ cup sugar and 1 to 2 drops of yellow food coloring. Mix red and blue food coloring together to create purple and mix in a jar with the remaining $\frac{1}{2}$ cup sugar. Sprinkle the colored sugars over the icing on the cake. Serve at room temperature.

MARDI GRAS

Mardi Gras, or Fat Tuesday in French, is the day before Ash Wednesday, when the Lenten season of austerity begins. It is a day of huge, blow-out festivities in New Orleans, a time of revelry, parades with floats, outrageous costumes, music, dancing in the streets, and presents for all—or at least for those lucky enough, or strong enough, to grab something, maybe a trinket, maybe a treasure, as it flies off a float. The week leading up to this day is one big party. Actually, the festivities begin much earlier, in January, with parades and parties—and King Cakes. The cakes, French in origin, are important not just because they are a tradition, but because the person whose piece of cake contains the "baby," a tiny toy doll or other small item, is designated host of the next party. And thus the tradition is continued.

This rich, delightful cheesecake dessert is unusual because it is made with tangy chèvre-style goat cheese. Firefly Farms is located near the headwaters of the Potomac River, one of the major tributaries of the Chesapeake Bay. They are among a small group of artisan cheese makers. The owners, Mike Koch and Pablo Solanet, started out with a small herd of goats—Nubian and Saanen—on a 130-acre farm, and in a matter of two years had won prestigious awards for their cheeses from the American Cheese Society. In addition to playing nanny to all the "kids," Pablo is a trained chef and created this marvelous cheesecake.

Firefly Farms Goat Cheese Cheesecake with Caramel Sauce

Makes 12

2^1/$_4$ cups graham cracker crumbs
^{1}/$_2$ cup coarsely chopped English walnuts
^{1}/$_2$ cup melted butter
Three 8-ounce packages cream cheese, at room temperature
8 ounces chèvre goat cheese, at room temperature
1^1/$_2$ cups sugar
1 cup sour cream
3 eggs
1 tablespoon cornstarch
^{1}/$_4$ cup heavy cream
1 teaspoon vanilla
Topping (recipe follows)

Preheat the oven to 350°F.

In a mixing bowl, combine 2 cups of the graham cracker crumbs, the English walnuts, and the butter. Press the mixture into the bottom and slightly up the sides of a 10-inch springform pan.

In a food processor, combine the cream cheese, goat cheese, sugar, and sour cream and blend until smooth. Add the eggs, one at a time, until incorporated.

Dissolve the cornstarch in the cream and add to the cheese mixture. Fold in the vanilla.

Pour the filling into the pan and bake for 50 minutes or until the cake has set. After removing the pan from the oven, run a knife around the edge to prevent the cake from cracking. Place on a wire rack to cool.

After the cake has cooled, spread the topping evenly over the top. Sprinkle with the remaining ^{1}/$_4$ cup of graham cracker crumbs and serve.

Topping

¹/₄ cup sour cream
¹/₄ cup chèvre goat cheese, at
room temperature
3 tablespoons honey
1 cup jarred caramel sauce
1 cup coarsely chopped
English walnuts

Combine all the ingredients and mix until smooth.

Coastal cheesecake, you ask? Ask no further than Ms. Edie Greenberg of San Diego, California. Edie is a whiz with Californian seafood, and people flock to her cooking classes. Edie says the fish stuff is fine, but she always likes to end the lesson on a sweet note.

Chocolate Velvet Cheesecake

Serves 12 to 16

One 8$\frac{1}{2}$-ounce package
   chocolate wafer cookies
Pinch of salt
Pinch of cinnamon
7 tablespoons butter, melted
One 12-ounce bag semi-sweet
   chocolate chips
1$\frac{1}{2}$ pounds (24 ounces)
   cream cheese, at room
   temperature
1 cup sugar
4 eggs
3 cups whipping cream
1 teaspoon vanilla
1 tablespoon confectioners'
   sugar
1$\frac{1}{2}$ to 2 cups seasonal fruit,
   such as strawberries,
   cherries, or small mango
   slices

Crush the cookies to the consistency of meal. Add the salt, cinnamon, and 5 tablespoons of the butter. Mix well and press firmly into a 12-inch springform pan. Chill for 30 minutes.

Preheat the oven to 350°F.

Melt the chocolate chips in the top half of a double boiler over low heat, stirring constantly. Remove from the heat.

In a food processor, beat the cream cheese with the sugar until fluffy. Add the eggs, one at a time, just incorporating each before adding another. Pour into a large bowl and whisk in the melted chocolate, the remaining 2 tablespoons butter, 2 cups whipping cream, and the vanilla.

Pour the batter into the springform pan and smooth the top. Bake for 45 to 60 minutes, or until the sides are firm. The center will still seem loose. Cool to room temperature on a wire rack, then chill in the springform pan overnight. To serve, whip the remaining cup of cream with the confectioners' sugar until it forms soft peaks. Pipe or dollop a bit of whipped cream onto each slice of cheesecake, and top with a bit of fruit. (The cheesecake can be frozen and topped when thawed.)

My friends Steve Hammond and Jackie Jackson, of Crofton, Maryland, are big fans of Hawaii, and go there every chance they get. They once spent a week on Maui and put 1,200 miles on their rental car just driving around looking at the stunning scenery and taking pictures of double rainbows. In their travels, they discovered a simple pineapple dessert and asked me to recreate it for them. This recipe is similar to the Amish dish called "Dutch babies"—a sort of rich, dense egg custard—but with pineapple juice added near the end of the baking process.

Haleakala Pineapple "Pan" Cake

Serves 4

1 1/4 cups all-purpose flour
1 tablespoon sugar
1/2 teaspoon salt
1/8 teaspoon freshly ground nutmeg
7 eggs, lightly beaten
1 1/4 cups milk
8 tablespoons (1 stick) butter
4 tablespoons pineapple juice
Pineapple-Rum Sauce (recipe follows)

Preheat the oven to 450°F.

In a large bowl, mix together the flour, sugar, salt, and nutmeg. In another bowl, mix the eggs and milk together and add to the flour mixture. Stir until blended but still slightly lumpy.

Melt the butter in the oven in a large glass baking dish or large cast-iron skillet. When the butter is bubbly, pour in the batter and bake for 20 minutes. Remove from the oven and pour the pineapple juice over the cake. Reduce the oven temperature to 350°F and return the cake to the oven for 10 more minutes. Serve immediately with Pineapple-Rum Sauce.

Pineapple-Rum Sauce

4 tablespoons (1/2 stick) butter
1/2 cup firmly packed brown sugar
1/2 teaspoon cinnamon
2 cups chopped fresh pineapple
2 tablespoons dark rum

Melt the butter in a saucepan over low heat. Add the brown sugar and cook, stirring, until the sugar melts. Add the cinnamon and the pineapple and sauté for about 5 minutes. Pour in the rum, raise the heat to medium-high, and cook, still stirring, for 2 to 3 minutes. Allow the sauce to cool slightly before spooning it over the cake.

As one travels below the Mason-Dixon Line, strawberry shortcake gives way to the Deep South's romance with juicy local peaches and just-off-the-tree pecans. When my Aunt Minnie's naval commander husband returned from a long voyage, she welcomed him home with his beloved breakfast biscuits, which she would also occasionally use to make a shortcake. The caramel in the candied pecans adds an extra dimension of flavor, but if you don't want to take the extra step of candying the pecans, add toasted nuts instead.

Peach Shortcake with Fluffy Cornmeal Pecan Topping

Serves 8 to 10

6 cups peaches, pitted and
    sliced, or two 16-ounce
    bags frozen slices, thawed
$1/4$ cup sugar
$1/4$ cup firmly packed light
    brown sugar
$1/2$ teaspoon cinnamon
2 tablespoons all-purpose
    flour
Pinch of salt
1 tablespoon butter, cut in
    small pieces
Fluffy Cornmeal Pecan
    Biscuit Dough (recipe
    follows)

Preheat the oven to 350°F.

Toss the peaches in a large bowl with the sugar, brown sugar, cinnamon, flour, and salt. Pour the peach mixture into a 9-inch deep-dish pie pan or a square baking dish. Dot the top with the butter. Bake for 30 minutes, until peaches are tender. Remove from the oven. Increase temperature to 400°F. Spread the biscuit dough rounds over the top—the covering doesn't have to be neat, and all the fruit doesn't have to be covered. Bake 10 to 12 minutes, or until the pastry is nicely browned and the fruit filling is bubbling. Remove from the oven to cool on a rack.

Fluffy Cornmeal Pecan Biscuit Dough

2 cups all-purpose flour, or
    more as needed
1 cup fine-ground white or
    yellow cornmeal
4 teaspoons baking powder
1 teaspoon salt
1 teaspoon sugar
$^1/_4$ teaspoon cream of tartar
$^1/_4$ cup vegetable shortening
4 tablespoons ($^1/_2$ stick)
    butter, cut into small
    pieces
8 to 10 tablespoons milk
1 cup candied pecan pieces
    (see note)

Sift together the flour, cornmeal, baking powder, salt, sugar, and cream of tartar in a mixing bowl. Cut in the shortening and butter with a fork, pastry blender, or your fingers until the mixture resembles coarse meal. Add 8 tablespoons of the milk, stirring until a stiff batter forms. Fold in the candied pecan pieces. If the batter is too dry, add a little more milk, one tablespoon at a time. Don't use more than 10 tablespoons.

Form the dough into a ball, wrap in plastic, and chill the dough for at least 30 minutes. When ready to use, unwrap the dough and roll it out on a lightly floured surface to about $^1/_2$ inch thick. Cut into rounds with a 2-inch biscuit cutter.

NOTE: To candy the pecans, melt 1 cup of sugar in a heavy-bottomed saucepan over high heat, stirring with a wooden spoon. When the sugar starts to darken, lower the heat and add 1 cup of pecan pieces and stir to coat thoroughly, cooking for another 30 seconds. Spread the mixture onto a greased baking sheet and set aside to cool and harden. When the mixture is cool, break it into small bits. You can use a food processor to do this, but don't over-process; you want small chunks, not crumbs or dust.

Janie Hibler, whose most recent book is The Berry Bible, *is Queen of the Berries in Portland, Oregon. Marionberries were developed in Oregon in 1956, and are a cross between two blackberries. They have small seeds and a rich, tart taste. A noted author and expert on the cuisine of the Pacific Northwest, Janie got this recipe from her friend Kathy Allcock, who got it from her grandmother, who got it from "an older woman from across the street." And that's the beauty of these traditional recipes: They connect generations and neighbors, and continue to be passed on.*

Cannon Beach Marionberry Cobbler

Serves 8 to 10

1 cup all-purpose flour
1 to 1$^{1}/_{2}$ cups sugar
$^{1}/_{2}$ teaspoon baking powder
2 tablespoons unsalted butter, softened
$^{2}/_{3}$ cup milk
1 pint (2 cups) fresh Marionberries, or 2 cups frozen Marionberries, thawed in a single layer on a paper towel for 20 minutes

Kathy's family made this cobbler every summer with blackberries picked at Cannon Beach, in far northwestern Oregon. Janie points out this is an unusual recipe because all the ingredients are mixed together and put into a buttered baking pan, then a cup of hot water is poured over the top. "As the batter cooks, it absorbs the water while rising to the surface, producing a memorable moist and berry-laden cobbler that just begs for some good old-fashioned vanilla ice cream to go with it."

If you can't find Marionberries fresh or frozen, you can substitute blackberries, raspberries, blueberries, or other fruit.

Preheat the oven to 350°F. Grease an 8 x 8-inch baking dish.

Stir together the flour, $^{1}/_{2}$ cup of the sugar, and the baking powder. Mix together the butter and the milk and stir into the dry ingredients. Toss the berries with $^{1}/_{2}$ to 1 cup sugar to taste, and stir into the batter.

Spoon the batter into the prepared baking dish. Pour 1 cup of hot water over all and bake for 45 minutes (50 minutes for frozen berries), until the batter rises to the surface around the edges of the pan and is light golden brown. Serve warm or at room temperature.

This is an old-fashioned coastal dessert that was originally baked overnight in the embers of the kitchen fireplace and eaten the next morning for breakfast. Nobody knows where the name comes from, but my friend Joanne Pritchett says that her grandmother claims the pandowdy is mighty good eating, even if it looks downright dowdy. I wouldn't even think of eating this dessert without a big scoop of vanilla ice cream—even at breakfast.

Apple-Apricot Pandowdy

Serves 8

2 tablespoons butter
5 cups (4 to 5) Gala or other cooking apples, peeled, quartered, cored, and thinly sliced
1 cup (3 to 4) pitted and sliced apricots
1 tablespoon lemon juice
3/4 cup firmly packed brown sugar, or 1/2 cup maple syrup
1 Sweet Flaky Pastry Crust (recipe follows)
1 tablespoon sugar
1/2 teaspoon cinnamon

Preheat the oven to 375°F. Use 1 tablespoon of the butter to grease an 8- or 9-inch baking dish.

In a mixing bowl, toss the fruit first with the lemon juice, then with the brown sugar or maple syrup. Pour the fruit into the prepared pan.

Roll out the pastry to a diameter of about 9 to 10 inches and place the pastry over the fruit, tucking the edges down around the filling. Cut the remaining tablespoon of butter in small pieces and dot the top of the pastry. Mix together the sugar and the cinnamon and sprinkle over the pastry.

Bake for about 30 minutes, or until the crust is golden. Remove from the oven, and using a sharp knife, score the crust diagonally into diamond shapes, about two inches wide. Use a spatula to press the crust down gently into the fruit. Return to the oven and bake until the crust is browned, about 15 minutes more. Remove from the oven and serve warm.

Sweet Flaky Pastry Crust

2 cups all-purpose flour
$^1/_2$ teaspoon salt
1 teaspoon sugar
8 tablespoons (1 stick) butter,
    cut into very small pieces
2 tablespoons vegetable
    shortening
$^1/_4$ cup ice water

Sift together the flour, salt, and sugar into a mixing bowl. Use a pastry blender or your fingers to work the butter and shortening into the flour mixture until it is the consistency of coarse meal. Add ice water, 1 tablespoon at a time, mixing with a fork after each addition. Add only enough water to make the dough stick together, about $^1/_4$ cup. When you can form the dough into a ball, wrap it in plastic wrap and refrigerate for at least 1 hour before using.

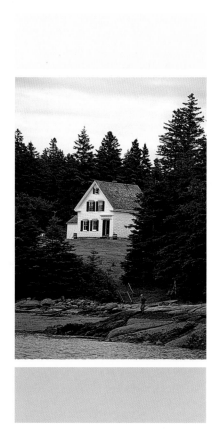

There are several variations on this classic Key West favorite. Some versions use a pastry crust, some use a graham cracker crust, some use a cookie-crumb crust. Sometimes the pie is topped with baked meringue and sometimes with whipped cream. This rich version pairs the tangy lime filling with a buttery chocolate crust, and tops it all off with whipped cream. Key limes, which are smaller and more acidic than regular limes, are extremely hard to find outside of southern Florida. Often you can find the Key lime juice bottled, but it's fine to use fresh regular limes.

Key Lime Pie

Serves 8 to 10

One 14-ounce can sweetened condensed milk
4 large egg yolks
$1/3$ cup strained Key lime juice
1 Cookie-Crumb Crust (recipe follows), baked
1 cup cold whipping cream
4 tablespoons confectioners' sugar
Zest of 1 lime, grated

Preheat the oven to 325°F.

In a large mixing bowl, whisk together the condensed milk, egg yolks, and lime juice until thick. Pour into the baked crust and place in the center of the oven. Bake for 10 to 15 minutes, or until the center is just set but still jiggly, like gelatin. Remove from the oven and cool to room temperature on a wire rack. Refrigerate until just before serving.

Meanwhile, beat the whipping cream and confectioners' sugar until the mixture forms soft peaks. Spread the whipped cream over the chilled pie and sprinkle with grated lime zest.

Cookie-Crumb Crust

1^1/2 cups fine chocolate wafer
    crumbs
4 tablespoons sugar
6 tablespoons butter, melted

Preheat the oven to 350°F.

Crumble the cookies into the bowl of a food processor, add the sugar, and pulse. Add the melted butter, and process until the cookies are in fine crumbs and are moist. (Or you can place cookies in a paper bag and roll with a rolling pin until desired consistency is reached. Mix crumbs, sugar, and melted butter in a bowl until blended.) Press the mixture into the bottom and up the sides of a 9-inch pie pan. Bake in the center of the oven for about 10 minutes, or until firm to the touch.

KEY LIMES Contrary to what you might think, Key limes not only are not exclusive to Key West, they're not even native to the Florida Keys. They are, in fact, the "original" lime, which originated in Southeast Asia (Malaysia or Indonesia). They were carried to the eastern Mediterranean by Arab traders, to Europe by the Crusaders, and to the West Indies by Christopher Columbus. They were grown commercially in Florida for a while, then a hurricane in the mid-1920s wiped out the orchards. The acreage was replanted with the sturdier Persian lime, which was developed earlier in the century. Commercial Key lime production in Florida is extremely limited, though Key limes are being grown in other states, notably Texas and California. (There's that coastal link again.) Key limes are smaller than Persian limes, and much thinner skinned. They're more acidic than Persian limes, though both varieties are more acidic than lemons. Bottled Key lime juice, made from imported concentrate, is available almost everywhere.

This classic dish is a bit of a fraud: In the first place, it's not a pie. In the second place, it's just a dressed-up version of an older recipe, called Boston Favorite Cake. Some clever chef cut the original basic cake into two layers, filled it with pastry cream, and topped it with chocolate sauce.

Boston Cream Pie

Preheat the oven to 350°F. Butter and flour two 8-inch cake pans.

Serves 8 to 10

1 cup sugar
6 tablespoons butter, softened
2 eggs, separated
1½ teaspoons vanilla
1¾ cups cake flour
2 teaspoons baking powder
½ teaspoon salt
⅔ cup milk
1½ cups Pastry Cream (recipe follows)
Dark Chocolate Sauce (recipe follows)

Place the sugar in the bowl of a mixer and beat in the butter, 1 tablespoon at a time, until the mixture is light and fluffy. Add the egg yolks and the vanilla and beat well.

Sift the flour with the baking powder and salt into a bowl, or over a sheet of wax paper.

Add about ½ cup of the flour mixture to the butter mixture and blend. Add ⅓ cup of the milk and blend. Repeat with next ½ cup of flour mixture and next ⅓ cup of milk, and finish with remaining flour mixture and remaining milk, beating until smooth.

In a clean mixing bowl, beat the egg whites until they form firm, but not stiff, peaks. Fold about one-third of the egg whites into the butter-flour mixture, then fold in the rest.

Pour the batter into the prepared pans and bake for 25 to 35 minutes, or until a toothpick inserted into the center of the cake comes out clean. Allow the layers to cool a few minutes in the pans, then run a thin, sharp knife around the edges of the pans and turn the layers out onto wire racks. Cool to room temperature.

Place one cake layer on a plate and top with chilled Pastry Cream. Place the second layer on top and drizzle warm Dark Chocolate Sauce over the top.

Pastry Cream

2 cups milk
5 egg yolks
6 tablespoons sugar
1$\frac{1}{2}$ tablespoons flour
1 tablespoon cornstarch
2 tablespoons vanilla

Heat the milk in a saucepan until hot. Place the egg yolks, sugar, flour, and cornstarch in a bowl and whisk until well blended. Slowly whisk in the hot milk. Pour the mixture into a clean saucepan over medium heat and cook, stirring constantly with a wooden spoon, until it comes to a boil. Boil for 1 minute, continuing to stir. Add the vanilla. Cool, cover, and chill in the refrigerator for at least 3 hours. The pastry cream can be made a day ahead.

Dark Chocolate Sauce

6 ounces dark chocolate
(semi-sweet or bittersweet),
cut in pieces
6 tablespoons milk
Pinch of salt
6 tablespoons unsalted butter

Put the chocolate, milk, and salt in the top half of a double boiler and heat, stirring frequently, until the chocolate is melted. Remove from the heat and add the butter, 1 tablespoon at a time, stirring until incorporated. Drizzle the sauce over the cake while still warm.

When I first entered the culinary world, quite a few crab cakes ago, one of my first chefs, Bert Katzen, a very kind and patient man, introduced me to my very first Bananas Foster. I thought it was the most amazing thing I'd ever seen—or tasted. I still love it.

Hotsy-Totsy Bananas Foster

The dramatic and old-fashioned dish is associated with the famous Brennan's restaurant in the French Quarter of New Orleans. This updated version has a little extra kick of heat besides the flames.

Traditionally, the dish is prepared at tableside over a spirit burner, with diners oohing and aahing over the blue flames. If you like a bit of theater with your dessert, you can try it—carefully. Flaming burns off the alcohol and softens the flavors, though some liquor will remain.

Serves 4

3 tablespoons butter
$^1/_2$ cup brown sugar
$^1/_4$ to $^1/_2$ teaspoon cinnamon
$^1/_8$ teaspoon nutmeg
$^1/_8$ teaspoon cayenne pepper
4 firm, ripe bananas, cut in half lengthwise, each piece cut in two
$^1/_2$ cup dark rum
4 tablespoons brandy or banana liqueur (optional)
4 scoops French vanilla ice cream
1 teaspoon confectioners' sugar

Melt the butter in a skillet. Stir in the sugar, cinnamon, nutmeg, and cayenne. Stir to mix and heat through. Add the bananas and sauté until they are soft and slightly browned.

Heat the rum and brandy, if using, in a small saucepan, then add to the skillet. When the spirits are hot, use a long fireplace match to set them aflame. Let the flames die down and remove the skillet from the heat.

Divide the ice cream among 4 plates and gently place 4 pieces of banana on top of each scoop. Spoon the sauce over the bananas and sprinkle with the confectioners' sugar. Serve at once.

Most rational persons consider pie a dessert, but for some reason I like a generous slice of pie—just about any kind—for breakfast, along with a fresh cup of coffee. This traditional pie is dark and rich and fragrant, like the native nuts that flavor it.

Southern Pecan Pie

Pecans are grown all over the southern coastal states, from North Carolina down to Atlantic Florida, and from the Gulf of Florida over to Texas. The biggest crop comes from Alabama.

Serves 8 to 10

One 9-inch Pie Crust (recipe follows)
3 large eggs
1 cup dark corn syrup
$^1/_2$ cup firmly packed dark brown sugar
4 tablespoons ($^1/_2$ stick) butter, melted
$^1/_2$ teaspoon salt
1 teaspoon vanilla
$1^1/_4$ cup pecans, halves or chopped (see note)
1 cup whipping cream

Preheat the oven to 375°F.

Prepare pie crust.

In a mixing bowl, combine the eggs, corn syrup, brown sugar, melted butter, salt, and vanilla. Mix together gently with a wire whisk until blended. Fold in the pecans and pour the filling into the prepared crust. Bake for 40 to 45 minutes, or until the crust is golden brown and the center of the pie is just set, but not hard—do not overbake, as that will make the filling gummy. Allow the pie to cool somewhat, or to room temperature, before serving. Whip the cream until it forms gentle peaks and add a dollop on each slice of pie.

NOTE: Pecan halves look prettier but make it harder to cut neat slices. If you like, you can use a mixture of chopped pecans and a few distinctive halves.

Pie Crust

Makes one 9-inch crust
1 1/2 cups all-purpose flour
3/4 teaspoon salt
1/2 cup solid shortening

Place a couple of ice cubes in a 1-cup measure and fill with water. Set aside.

In a mixing bowl, combine the flour and salt. Add the shortening and use a fork to press the shortening into the flour mixture until it is crumbly. Work quickly and carefully, and do not overwork the dough, as it will become tough.

Add 2 tablespoons of ice-cold water to the bowl and, still using the fork, incorporate it into the flour-shortening mixture.

Squeeze a small handful of the dough to see if it forms a ball. You want to add only enough water to make the dough hold together for rolling out, and not a drop more. The less water you use and the less you work the dough, the flakier your crust will be. If the dough is still too crumbly with 2 tablespoons of water, add one more and incorporate and do the squeeze test again. You should not need to add more than 4 tablespoons of water.

Form the crust into a ball and roll out on a pastry surface or between two sheets of wax paper to a diameter of 9 inches. Place in the pie pan and press to the surface. Fold and crimp the rim attractively.

Rice was one of the first commercial crops grown in the Carolinas during Colonial times, and it is, pardon the pun, ingrained in the area's cuisine, being served for breakfast, lunch, and dinner. There are two basic schools of thought about preparing rice pudding. One version is cooked and served from the pot, and the other is cooked briefly in the pot and then transferred to the oven and baked, giving a firmer consistency. The baked version is usually served with cream. This recipe has a creamy texture, along with a shot of very "Southern" hooch for that extra bit of comfort in a cold world.

Comforting Carolina Rice Pudding with Roasted Pine Nuts

Serves 6

$^1/_3$ cup medium-grain rice
4 cups milk
$^1/_4$ teaspoon salt
2 egg yolks
$^3/_4$ cup sugar
$^1/_4$ teaspoon nutmeg
1 teaspoon grated lemon zest
$^1/_2$ teaspoon cinnamon
1 teaspoon vanilla
$1^1/_2$ teaspoons Southern
    Comfort, optional
Cinnamon, for garnish
$^1/_2$ cup roasted pine nuts, for
    garnish (see note)

Put the rice, milk, and salt into a saucepan and bring to a boil. Reduce heat to low and simmer, partially covered, for 40 minutes. In a bowl, whisk together the egg yolks and the sugar until well blended and add to the rice mixture, along with the nutmeg, lemon zest, cinnamon, vanilla, and Southern Comfort. Raise the heat and cook, bring back to a boil, stirring constantly, for 1 minute.

Pour into individual serving dishes and cool to warm. (Pudding will thicken some as it sits.) Sprinkle with cinnamon and pine nuts and serve warm, or sprinkle with cinnamon and chill. If serving chilled, just before serving, sprinkle with the pine nuts.

NOTE: To roast pine nuts, place them in a cast-iron or other heavy-bottomed skillet over medium-high heat. Cook the nuts, stirring constantly, until all are golden brown, 2 to 3 minutes.

Comfort and hospitality are the foundations of island life. A lot of Hawaiian food might be called comfort food, such as poi, noodle and rice dishes, and this traditional coconut pudding. This particular version adds a little toasted coconut for crunch.

Crispy-Creamy Hawaiian Coconut Pudding

Serves 6

One 13 1/2-ounce can
  unsweetened coconut milk
One 12-ounce can evaporated
  milk
7 tablespoons cornstarch
6 tablespoons sugar
1 1/2 cups sweetened flaked or
  shredded coconut, toasted
  (see note)

Put the coconut milk and evaporated milk in the top of a double boiler. Thoroughly mix 1/2 cup water with the cornstarch and add to the milks. Add the sugar. Cook over medium heat, stirring frequently, until thick. Fold in 3/4 cup of the toasted coconut. Transfer to individual serving dishes and refrigerate until well chilled. Top with the rest of the toasted coconut before serving.

NOTE: To toast coconut, preheat the oven to 350°F. Spread the coconut on a baking sheet and bake for 8 to 10 minutes, stirring frequently, until lightly browned.

PET MILK   It started in the 1880s in Highland, Illinois, when a young immigrant from Switzerland offered the town people a business proposal: If they would invest $15,000 in his plant to produce shelf-stable "evaporated," or condensed, milk, they would profit beyond their wildest dreams. They didn't, at least not right away, because after only a few years, the company had to be shut down because of a spoilage problem. When that was resolved, the company slowly but surely took off. The milk was popular in parts of the West where there wasn't much fresh milk; in hotter climates, such as coastal Texas and Louisiana, where the weather made keeping fresh milk difficult; and as a safe baby food. Pet astutely made its condensed milk standard fare for soldiers, starting with the Spanish-American War. In 1933, Pet went on the radio with a fifteen-minute program that included household hints, meal plans, and, of course, recipes featuring Pet Milk. Some of those recipes are still lurking in the recipe collections of Baby Boomers, whose mothers raised them on the stuff.

Dulce de leche (sweet milk), a traditional Hispanic dessertlike spread, sometimes called "milk jam," requires caramelizing milk for many hours to make the luscious, sweetened, thickened milk sauce. Thankfully, it is available in Hispanic markets and specialty food shops.

Dulce de Leche Bread Pudding

Michelle Bernstein, a favorite chef in Miami, Florida, uses dulce de leche to create a new dimension in comfort food. The recipe, theoretically enough for four people, is so good, I might only invite one other person to join me.

Serves 4

2 cups milk

3 eggs, beaten

$^1/_3$ cup sugar

$^1/_2$ teaspoon salt

$^1/_2$ teaspoon vanilla extract

Four 1-inch-thick slices white
  bread, crusts removed

$^3/_4$ cup dulce de leche (see
  page 276)

$^1/_2$ cup raisins steeped in
  $^1/_2$ cup hot rum

1 teaspoon cinnamon

Dash of nutmeg

Preheat the oven to 350°F. Butter an 8 x 8-inch baking dish.

In a saucepan, heat the milk over low heat until hot, but not boiling. In a large bowl, combine the eggs, sugar, and salt; stir well. Gradually stir in about $^1/_4$ of the hot milk to the egg mixture. Add the remaining milk, stirring constantly. Stir in vanilla.

Place the bread slices in the baking dish. Spread them with the dulce de leche. Sprinkle raisins over the bread. Pour the milk mixture over the bread. Combine the cinnamon and nutmeg and sprinkle over the pudding mixture. Bake, uncovered, for 40 to 45 minutes, or until the edges are set. Serve warm.

I love this dessert and Miss Daisy. This is a French coastal dessert that has made its way from St. Tropez in France to St. Bart's in the Caribbean, and finally to the shores of the Chesapeake via Miss Daisy Lenoble. Daisy tells me the recipe was actually developed by her grandmother in France and has been a hit everywhere she has served it to guests. Nougatine is a candied dessert, made with some type of nut, and glacé refers to ice cream or frozen dessert. Put them together and voilà, you have my all-time favorite dessert.

Miss Daisy's Nougatine Glacé with Berries

Serves 8 to 10

2 cups heavy whipping cream
1 cup sugar
$1/4$ cup corn syrup
6 egg whites
Almond Praline (recipe follows)
Fresh Berry Sauce (recipe follows)
1 pint fresh berries, e.g., blackberries, raspberries, blueberries, strawberries, or a combination thereof

Place a metal mixing bowl in the freezer to chill for at least $1/2$ hour. Whip the cream in the prechilled bowl until soft yet somewhat firm peaks form. Set aside.

In a saucepan, combine the sugar, corn syrup, and $1/2$ cup water. Bring to a boil over high heat until the mixture reaches 240°F on a candy thermometer.

In a large mixing bowl, whip the egg whites with an electric mixer until firm and shiny. Very slowly add the sugar mixture and gently incorporate it until the sides of the bowl are cool to the touch. Gently fold in the Almond Praline and then fold in the whipped cream. Spoon the mixture into small plastic drinking cups or custard molds, cover with plastic, and place in the freezer until firm.

When ready to serve, remove the cups or molds from the freezer and allow them to sit at room temperature for about 5 minutes. Run a thin knife that has been dipped in hot water around the edges of the molds. Invert onto serving plates and garnish with Fresh Berry Sauce and the fresh berries.

Almond Praline

2 cups blanched, sliced
  almonds
1 cup sugar
1/4 cup light corn syrup

Preheat the oven to 400°F.

Spread out the almonds on a rimmed baking sheet and toast in the oven until lightly browned, 3 to 4 minutes. Set aside.

In a saucepan, mix the sugar, corn syrup, and 1/2 cup water. Bring to a boil over high heat and continue cooking until the mixture reaches 340°F on a candy thermometer.

Pour the syrup mixture over the nuts and spread out evenly on the baking sheet. Allow to cool completely. When cooled, break praline into pieces and finely chop in a food processor.

Fresh Berry Sauce

1 pint strawberries or
  raspberries
1/4 cup sugar

Rinse the berries in a colander and set aside. Bring the sugar and 1/2 cup water to a boil in a saucepan and cook for 1 minute. Let cool. Place the berries in a blender or food processor. Add the sugar water and puree. Pass the mixture through a fine strainer to remove the seeds. Refrigerate until ready to use.

The Coastal Cooking Resource Guide

Popular Seafood in Coastal Regions

NEW ENGLAND

SHELLFISH

Lobster

Mussels

Sea Scallops

Bay Scallops

Hard Clams

Soft-Shell Clams

FISH

Cod

Scrod (smaller cod)

Haddock

Flounder

Halibut

Atlantic Salmon

Squid

Mackerel

MID-ATLANTIC

SHELLFISH

Blue Crab

Soft-Shell Crab

Oysters

Hard Clams

Soft-Shell Clams

FISH

Rockfish (Striped Bass)

Bluefish

Catfish

Flounder

Perch

Shad

Shad Roe

Herring

CAROLINAS TO KEY WEST

SHELLFISH

Blue Crab

Shrimp (brown, pink, and white)

Oysters

Hard Clams

Sea Scallops

Stone Crab

FISH

Flounder

Atlantic Croaker

Yellowfin Tuna

King Mackerel

Red Snapper

Pompano

Black Sea Bass

Grouper

Catfish

THE GULF COAST

SHELLFISH

Shrimp
Oysters
Blue Crab
Crayfish

FISH

Grouper
Red Drum
Black Drum
Red Snapper
Flounder

CALIFORNIA

SHELLFISH

Dungeness Crab
Oysters
Clams
Abalone
Shrimp
Crayfish

FISH

Sturgeon
Halibut
Striped Bass
Tilefish
Skate
Squid
Octopus
Sole
Sandabs
Tuna
Swordfish

PACIFIC NORTHWEST

SHELLFISH

Oysters
Mussels
Clams
Scallops
Dungeness Crab
Snow Crab

FISH

Halibut
Chinook Salmon
Coho Salmon
Sockeye Salmon
Ocean Perch
Ling Cod
Rockfish
Squid
Octopus

HAWAII

FISH

Tuna Family
  Ahi
  Bigeye
  Tombo
  Yellowfin
Spearfish
Pacific Blue Marlin
Swordfish
Mahi Mahi
Ono
Opah (Moonfish)
Grouper
Snapper

Food Resource References

The list below is in no way meant to be a definitive coastal food guide, but rather to provide contact information on some of the food products referred to in this book.

Amigo Foods—Web-based Hispanic/Latin American grocer.
www.amigofoods.com

Asian Food Grocer—Web-based Asian foods.
www.asianfoodgrocer.com

Firefly Farms—Artisan-crafted goat cheese.
www.fireflyfarms.com

LNB Groves—Information on exotic tropical fruit from Florida.
25250 S.W. 194th Avenue, Homestead, Florida 33031
(305) 248-7595

Louisiana Foods—Cajun and Creole seasonings, crawfish, and cookware.
www.CajunGrocer.com

Penn Cove Shellfish—Information on farmed mussels and clams.
www.penncoveshellfish.com

Phillips Foods—Crabmeat and other seafood products.
www.phillipsfoods.com
(800) 782-CRAB (to order crabmeat)

Priester's Pecans—High-quality southern pecans.
www.priesterspecans.com

Seabolt's Smokehouse—Fine Pacific Northwest smoked salmon.
www.seabolts.com
(800) 574–1120

Sun Ray Seafood—To order fresh conch or find a local distributor.
15223 N.W. 60th Avenue, Hialeah, Florida 33014
(305) 819–8327

Tillamook Cheese Coop—A long-established Pacific Northwest cheese maker.
www.tillamookcheese.com
(503) 815–1300

32nd Street Farmers Market—This is where I shop every Saturday when I'm at
    home in Baltimore.
www.32ndstreetmarket.org

Index